100 MICRO
Amigurumi

Crochet patterns and charts for tiny amigurumi

STEFFI GLAVES

DAVID & CHARLES

www.davidandcharles.com

Contents

Introduction

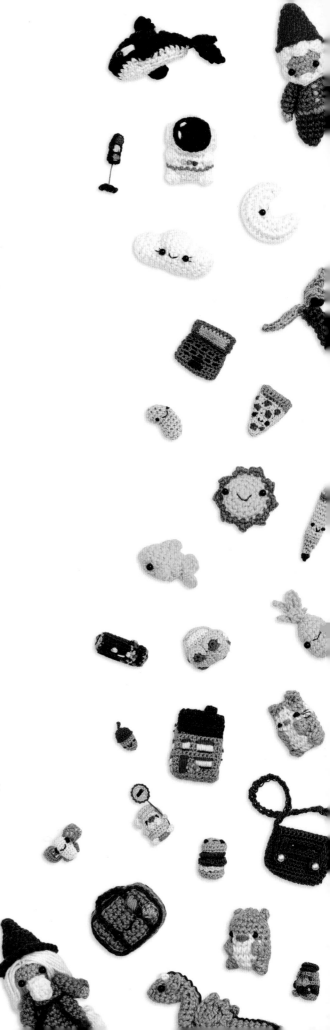

Amigurumi celebrates crochet's full potential to combine cuteness and character. Any object, from a piece of fruit to a traffic cone, can be given the amigurumi treatment, and once you've made your first pieces, you'll discover that the possible variations are endless. In fact, before you know it, you'll have run out of friends to give your creations to!

This book will introduce you to the amigurumi world on a miniature scale. You will find 100 micro amigurumi patterns which can be made as small as your thumbnail and can become charms, jewellery, keyrings, or perhaps doll's house decorations.

In the following ten chapters, you will discover some well-loved themes, as well as a few more unusual projects. Make your own mushroom sidekick, a tiny café, or even a miniature dragon. I loved designing each of these pieces and the imaginary worlds they inhabit, and I encourage you to do what I did while writing this book - look around, what can you see that could be transformed by amigurumi?

This book is for anyone who has a grasp of basic crochet stitches and has perhaps already explored a little amigurumi. Although the emphasis is on micro-crochet, all of the designs work with hooks and yarns of any size. If you have not crocheted such small pieces before, you can always start by working with your usual thread or yarn, and gradually scale down as you become more comfortable with the patterns. You will learn the skills needed for micro-crochet, such as how to hold your thread and hook, crocheting in rounds and embroidering faces, as well as different ways of stuffing your pieces to bring them to life.

My hope is that by the end of this book, you will have acquired the skills and confidence to make your own pieces so that your cast of amigurumi characters will be springing up around you. Or, rather, out of the end of your crochet hook!

Before You Begin

The amigurumis are split into ten chapters, each with its own distinct theme and possible applications. But before diving into the patterns, refer to this section for guidance on the tools and materials you will need for working micro-crochet. Have a look at the techniques section for some tips and tricks for making the most of these designs.

TOOLS & MATERIALS

Let's start by looking at the threads and yarns used in this book.

There are lots of different types of thread that are suitable for micro-crochet, varying in thickness and application, so you can slowly transition from crochet using standard yarns and hooks to using finer threads and hooks.

Here are the main things to look out for when purchasing your own threads.

THICKNESS/GAUGE NUMBER

Threads specifically made for fine crochet have a number to indicate the thickness or gauge. The higher the number, the finer the thread. Most common gauges are 10, 20, 30, 40, 50, 60, 70, 80 and 100. I use sewing cotton more than crochet cotton and use the equivalent of gauge 80 with a 0.5mm (12 steel) hook for most of my work. Common sewing threads will not have this numbering system.

MERCERISED

You will often see this on packaging for crochet threads. Mercerised cotton means that it has undergone a chemical and heat process to give it a lustre.

'Fibre halo' is particularly important if you are looking at sewing threads. Put a thread strand up to the light - do you see a halo of fibres around the main core of the thread? Most threads will have this, but too much will reduce the appearance of definition in the stitches of your work and make it prone to tangling.

STRENGTH

Even the finest of threads can be strong. If it snaps easily, then I wouldn't recommend crocheting with it. There is nothing worse than achieving the perfect magic ring, only for the tail end to snap off as you are drawing it to a close! This will not usually happen with specific crochet threads but there is a risk with sewing threads.

COLOUR RANGE

When looking at different ranges and brands of threads consider the following - does this brand have a range of colours that appeal to you? Can these threads be combined easily with others you have at home? There is nothing wrong with combining thread brands, though major differences in thread thickness may affect the overall look of your crochet pieces.

THREAD CLASSIFICATION

This book uses two brands of thread: Scheepjes Maxi yarn (the thickest) and Gütermann Top Stitching (the thin-side of middle) and Gütermann Hand Quilting (the thinnest) threads. There are lots of different types and brands of thread that you can enjoy making these patterns with, and I encourage you to try them all. But first, let's look at the ones I have used:

GÜTERMANN TOP STITCHING THREAD

This is a polyester thread which is great when trying out micro-crochet for the first time. Its proper purpose is for strong stitching on heavy duty fabrics such as denim. It is readily available in shops and is low in cost.

The hooks I use for this thread are a 0.75mm (14/10 steel) hook especially for amigurumi but a 0.9mm-1mm (14/8 to 12/6 steel) can also be used.

GÜTERMANN HAND QUILTING COTTON

This is a very lightly waxed cotton which gives fantastic definition to the stitches and a little more strength. It is smooth, with a subtle sheen and low friction properties, which makes it great for tiny magic rings and it can be frogged multiple times without snagging or losing its appearance.

Though it is slightly expensive for 200m (220yd), a little goes a long way, and the threads are wound on a spool which have a hidden compartment for needles, making it suitable for travel without tangling.

The colour range is limited, compared to specialised crochet cottons, but it is more readily available in local haberdasheries. If you ever want to use this thread for sewing in other craft projects, do note that this thread is not suitable for use on a sewing machine, as the fine wax in the cotton can clog up the machine mechanisms.

I use a 0.5mm (12 steel) hook, but a 0.6mm (12 steel) hook can also be used.

When purchasing Gütermann threads, check that you have picked the right thread by looking at the colour of the reel. Hand quilting cotton, which is a pale off-pink coloured reel, can often be confused with machine quilting cotton which has a grey coloured reel. The top stitching thread is a bright pale green coloured reel and comes on a smaller 30-metre reel.

SCHEEPJES MAXI YARN

Scheepjes Maxi is a great introductory yarn for amigurumi. It is a lace-weight cotton that handles nicely if you're new to micro-crochet; it's mercerised with a high twist, which gives a nice definition to the stitches. It comes in lots of different colours that complement each other really well. It's an excellent yarn to have in your stash as it can be used in so many different projects, from clothing to interior decoration.

This particular type of cotton comes in different lengths per ball, so you can choose how much you need depending on your chosen projects:

Sweet Treat 25g, 140m (1oz, 153yd). The nice thing about micro-crochet is that you don't need an enormous amount of yarn, so I recommend this size.

Sugar Rush 50g, 280m (2oz, 306yd)

Maxi 100g, 560m (4oz, 613yd)

I recommend using a 1.25mm (9/4 steel) hook for these yarns. You can go up to a 1.5mm (8/7/2 steel) hook, but your amigurumis will have a different size and texture.

With the exception of Light Effects, the following types of cottons aren't used in the book, but can certainly be used and explored:

DMC

DMC has the widest range of crochet cottons and gauges, useful for those who want to gradually work down the thread and hook sizes.

Special Dentelles 80 is a fine 3-ply crochet cotton that has been combed, singed with a flame and twice mercerised. It has a lovely sheen and there are 72 colours to choose from. They are wound in adorable little balls but they can unravel easily, so I recommend storing them with bands or in individual bags. I use a 0.5mm/0.6mm (12 steel) hook to work with DMC, and it can be combined with Gütermann hand quilting cotton.

If you want to try thicker threads, DMC also have **Perlé** threads which have a bit more of a sheen and come in lots of beautiful colours, available wound and in mini-skeins. They produce size 12, which is the thinnest, pair with a 0.9mm-1mm (14/8 to 12/6 steel) hook; size 8, pair with a 1mm (12/6 steel) hook; and size 5, pair with a 1.25mm (9/4 steel) hook. They also stock **Petra**, which is available in different thicknesses, suitable for hooks from 1.5mm (8/7/2 steel) to 3.5mm (E4).

If you want to add metallic elements to your amigurumi, **Light Effects** is a lovely six-stranded thread by DMC that is nice for both embroidery and crochet.

EMBROIDERY THREADS

These are great to begin with as they are cheap, available in many colours, and may often be in your existing craft stash. Most embroidery threads are made up of six very thin strands which can be separated to create thinner threads. Starting off with embroidery threads is a good way to work out what sort of threads you are comfortable with and therefore which hook size. Both Anchor and DMC offer embroidery threads in a variety of lovely shades.

CROCHET HOOKS

Now let's move onto crochet hooks. There are a couple of things to bear in mind when choosing these.

HOOK SIZE VARIATIONS

You can choose hooks that are different in size to what is recommended in the table. When working at such a small scale, where the difference in hook sizes can be 0.1mm, there can be subtle differences from brand to brand. They can also differ in hook shape and curve, so it is important to consider different ones. For example, I use a 0.5mm hook for a gauge 80 crochet cotton as I have quite tight tension – you may prefer a 0.6mm hook.

In amigurumi, it is typical to use the smallest hook possible for the thread or yarn you are using, to ensure that the stitches are small and tight so that the stuffing doesn't come through. As there isn't as much stuffing in micro-crochet because they're so small, this isn't so much of an issue. Therefore, the most important thing you need to consider is choosing the hook that you are most comfortable with for the thread you are using.

HANDLES AND BRANDS

Some hooks are available with or without handles. I certainly recommend buying one with a handle for comfort. They come in different sizes, materials, shapes and textures. I use a **Clover Soft Touch**, which is flat with a grip pad. Clover also has the **Amour Soft Grip** range that has a rounder handle with a silicone grip. Another good brand is **Tulip** which offers **Etimo Steel** and **Etimo Rose** for a more ergonomic grip.

AVAILABILITY

It is always preferable to have a look at the hook in store rather than buying online, however, micro-crochet is not as commonly practised as regular crochet, so very small hooks are not always on the shelves in your local craft shop. If they stock brands such as Clover and Tulip, it is always worth asking if one can be ordered in for you – that is how I got my first micro-crochet hook!

The table shown here lists which hooks I use for which thread gauges. I have a tight tension, which is ideal for micro-crochet, so I prefer a finer hook. There is flexibility in going up or down a size depending on your preferred tension. If you feel that your tension is too tight, I recommend going up a hook size as you would with regular crochet.

Thread	UK Hook	US Hook
3	1.75 to 2mm (DMC recommends 3.5mm)	4/0 to 4 steel
5	1.25 to 1.5mm (DMC recommends 2.5mm)	9/4 to 8/7/2 steel
8	0.9mm to 1mm (DMC recommends 1.5mm)	14/8 to 12/6 steel
10	0.9mm to 1mm	14/8 to 12/6 steel
20	0.9mm	14/8 steel
30	0.9mm	14/8 steel
40	0.75mm to 0.9mm	14/10 to 14/8 steel
50	0.75mm	14/10 steel
60	0.75mm	14/10 steel
70	0.6mm	12 steel
80	0.5mm to 0.6mm	12 steel
Sewing threads	0.35mm to 0.5mm	12 steel

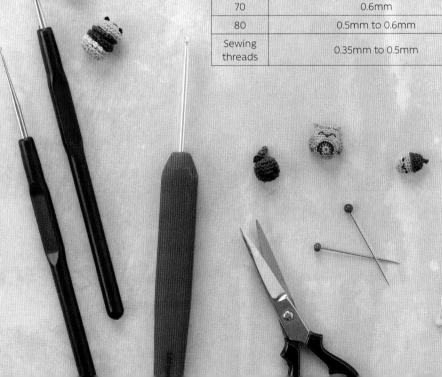

GENERAL TOOLS

Let's get into some tools you'll find useful, no matter how small or large you crochet.

NEEDLES

For the tiniest of stitches in sewing thread, I use John James bead embroidery needles in size 10. The eyes are very thin so won't disrupt your crochet stitches, but they're surprisingly strong. You certainly need a pin cushion because they will easily get lost in your carpet if you drop them. For thicker threads, you have more options for needles; look for the thickness of the eye compared to the needle shaft; the closer they are in width, the easier it will be to thread them through your work.

JEWELLERY PLIERS

For the odd occasion where your needle gets stuck sewing elements together, using pliers to pull the needle out of your work will save your hands some pain!

RUBBER THIMBLES

Rubber thimbles protect your fingers from the stabbiness of teeny tiny hooks. There are many different kinds available online that vary in size and thickness. I don't often wear one when crocheting, but I have found it quite a relief to wear one on my middle finger (on my non-hook hand) during long crochet sessions. The one I use is a finger cover for playing electric guitars. It protects my finger while being thin enough for it to not effect my dexterity, and I can still feel what is happening while I'm crocheting.

TWEEZERS

For stuffing, the thinner and pointier the better. If you don't have tweezers, you can use old sewing scissors instead.

SCISSORS

No craft stash is complete without your favourite pair of scissors. Make sure that they're small and sharp.

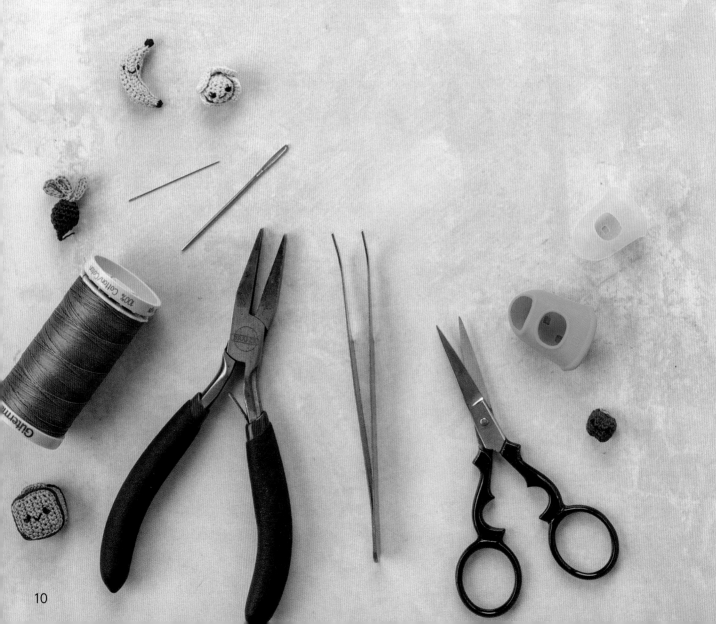

EYES

There are lots of options for safety eyes when working with regular DK or thicker yarns; they can range from 5mm-20mm in size. However, even 5mm is too big for working in micro-crochet, so here are a few alternatives that can look just as good.

PIN EYES

Pin eyes are typically used for making felted sculptures. They are made of glass or plastic and are mounted onto a soft wire. They can go as small as 1mm in size, but be warned that these are certainly not as secure as safety eyes, and are only suitable for ornamental purposes, not for toys. They will still be too big for crocheting with fine sewing threads and are more suitable for finger-weight yarns. See Finishing Techniques for methods that you can use to add them to your amigurumi.

BEADS

Beads are, in my opinion, the fuss-free alternative to safety eyes. The reason why I like them is that you can decide where they will be placed after finishing the amigurumi, rather than halfway through. When using beads, you can experiment with different placements on the face before fully committing. Here are my tips for choosing beads:

- Experiment with sizes: the smaller the face the smaller the beads, however 2mm is a good size for most amigurumi projects in this book.

- Don't go for seed beads. They're great for jewellery but they are not fully round, so can sit in an odd position on your amigurumi face. This creates the risk of making wonky eyes instead of cute eyes.

- Look at the hole size. The smaller the hole size the 'rounder' your beads will look, which is better for the amigurumi eye look.

For the amigurumis in this book I used 2mm round beads made from agate with the Scheepjes Sweet Treat cotton threads. Although it sounds unnecessarily fancy to use gemstone beads, they are milled to have a very small hole and have a very similar look to safety eyes. They are consistent in size and shape, unlike some packet beads you can buy, and they are often packed on a string so they can't be spilled or scattered like a regular tub of beads. The John James beading needles in size 10 are fine enough to use with them. They are available in many shops online but I bought mine from Amazon.

EMBROIDERY

Embroidery is best for the smallest of micro-crochet. It doesn't require any extra materials and you can use different types of stitches to create the look you want. I recommend you practise before you commit to your amigurumi, as mistakes are not easily undone – you would need to snip them off to remove.

Fairy Woodland

I don't think it matters how old we are, there will always be a need for a bit of forest magic in our lives. Look to your inner moss-cave-dwelling-craft-goblin and make a little mushroom or acorn companion, or tiny fairy cottage. These little characters would make excellent sidekicks to the fellows in the Myth & Legend chapter, just imagine the tiny owl resting in the wizard's beard!

This chapter uses a mix of Gütermann top stitching thread and hand quilting cotton, but you can change the threads and hooks to find a scale that suits you.

MUSHROOM

Materials

- 0.5mm-0.6mm (12 steel) crochet hook (0.6mm will produce slightly larger item)
- Gütermann hand quilting cotton in Ivory 919, Mid Red 2453, Black 5201, White 5709
- Embroidery needle

Finished Size

15mm x 13mm x 13mm (¹⁹⁄₃₂in x ³³⁄₆₄in x ³³⁄₆₄in)

Base

Special stitches: 5trBO – bobble stitch made with 5 tr sts, for feet (see Crochet Techniques)

For the base and underside of cap, work in continuous rounds, starting with a magic ring in Ivory.

Round 1: 8dc into ring (8 sts).

Round 2: 2dc in every st (16 sts).

Round 3: [Ss, 3ch, 5trBO, 3ch, ss] in first st (makes first foot), 2dc in each of next 4 sts, [ss, 3ch, 5trBO, 3ch, ss] in next st (makes second foot), [2dc in next st, 1dc] 5 times (23 dc and 2 bobble sts).

Round 4: 1dc in every st, including top of bobble sts (25 sts).

Rounds 5 to 8: 1dc in every st.

Round 9: [Dc2tog, 3dc] 5 times (20 sts).

Round 10: [Dc2tog, 3dc] 4 times (16 sts).

Round 11: 2BLdc in every st (32 sts).

Round 12: 1dc in every st.

Change to Mid Red.

Round 13: 1dc in every st.

Fasten off and stuff body.

Cap

Work in continuous rounds, starting with a magic ring in Mid Red.

Round 1: 8dc into ring (8 sts).

Round 2: 2dc in every st (16 sts).

Round 3: 1dc in every st.

Round 4: [2dc in next st, 1dc] 8 times (24 sts).

Round 5: [2dc in next st, 2dc] 8 times (32 sts).

Rounds 6 and 7: 1dc in every st.

Fasten off. Using White, embroider small patches on the cap.

Place cap on top of base, using Mid Red [ss, 1ch] in BL of each pair of sts to join, stuffing cap as you go. Embroider eyes using Black between rounds 5 and 6, 4 sts apart. Embroider mouth in between eyes using Black.

SPECKLE LOG

Materials

- 0.75mm-0.9mm (14/10 to 14/8 steel) crochet hook (0.9mm will produce slightly larger item)
- Gütermann top stitching thread in Light Brown 868, Dark Red 369, Mid Green 235, Dark Green 472, Light Green 152, Dusky Pink 473
- Embroidery needle

Finished Size

19mm x 15mm x 11mm (¾in x ¹⁹⁄₃₂in x ⁷⁄₁₆in)

Log Ends

Work the log ends in continuous rounds, starting with a magic ring in Light Brown.

Round 1: 6dc into ring (6 sts).

Round 2: 2dc in every st (12 sts).

Ss in next st and fasten off. Embroider a spiral in Dark Red.

Log Panel

Starting with Dark Red, make 11ch.

Row 1 (RS): Starting in second ch from hook, 1dc in every st (10 sts).

Rows 2 to 11: 1ch, turn, 1BLdc in every st.

Row 12: 1 BLdc in first 2 sts, [BLss, 2ch, 1BLhtr, 2ch, BLss] in next st, 1BLdc in rem 7 sts.

Fasten off, leaving a long thread for sewing.

Embroider details before sewing log panel together. Embroider leaves and branches with Mid Green and add French knots in Dark Green. Embroider eyes in Light Green on row 10, 3 sts apart and cheeks with Dusky Pink.

Whipstitch BLs of round 2 log ends to sides of panel, stuff, and sew BLs of row 12 to beg foundation ch row.

SNAIL

Materials

- 0.5mm-0.6mm (12 steel) crochet hook (0.6mm will produce slightly larger item)
- Gütermann hand quilting cotton in Light Grey 618, Dusky Pink 2635, Black 5201, Dark Red 2833
- Embroidery needle

Finished Size

15mm x 10mm x 21mm (¹⁹⁄₃₂in x ²⁵⁄₆₄in x ⁵³⁄₆₄in)

Shell

Work the shell in continuous rounds, starting with a magic ring in Dusky Pink.

Round 1: 8dc into ring (8 sts).

Round 2: 2dc in every st (16 sts).

Round 3: [2dc in next st, 1dc] 8 times (24 sts).

Round 4: 1dc in every st.

Round 5 (RS): 1BLdc in every st, do not ss to join (24 sts).

Rounds 6 to 8: 1ch, turn, 1dc in every st, makes top of shell with small slit for stuffing.

Round 9 (RS): 1ch, turn, 1BLdc in every st.

Round 10: Do not turn, [1dc, dc2tog] 8 times (16 sts).

Round 11: [Dc2tog] 8 times (8 sts).

Round 12: [2dc, dc2tog] twice (6 sts).

Fasten off and use the excess thread to sew the hole left after round 12 closed. Sew in remaining ends.

Swirl

Swirl can be worked using embroidery or surface crochet with Dark Red. Starting at round 1, work surface ss in a swirl up to round 4 then follow the BLs of round 5 to define the edge of the shell. Repeat on other side of shell.

Stuff through the slot made in rounds 6 to 8 then sew closed. Make sure this area is covered by the body when sewing together.

Body

Work in continuous rounds from tail to head, starting with a magic ring in Light Grey.

Round 1: 8dc into ring (8 sts).

Rounds 2 to 4: 1dc in every st.

Round 5: [2dc in next st, 3dc] twice (10 sts).

Rounds 6 and 7: 1dc in every st.

Round 8: [2dc in next st, 4dc] twice (12 sts).

Round 9: 1dc in every st.

Round 10: [2dc in next st, 5dc] twice (14 sts).

Round 11: 1dc in every st.

Round 12: [2dc in next st, 6dc] twice (16 sts).

Rounds 13 to 17: 1dc in every st.

Lightly stuff, making sure it is still flexible.

Joining and Eye Stalks

[Ss, 4ch, ss] in first st, hold both sides of last round together, [1ch, ss] in next 7 sts joining both sides, [ss, 4ch, ss] in last st, fasten off and sew in ends.

Embroider eyes onto 4ch loop in Black.

Sew body onto shell. Ensure shell opening is covered by body.

Antennae

These are best worked after finishing body for positioning.

9PCIC (see Crochet Techniques), fasten off. Thread through top of head between sts and sew into place.

ACORN

Materials

- 0.5mm-0.6mm (12 steel) crochet hook (0.6mm will produce slightly larger item)
- Gütermann hand quilting cotton in Fawn Brown 1225, Mid Brown 1833, Black 5201
- Embroidery needle

Finished Size

12mm x 6mm x 6mm (¹⁵⁄₃₂in x ¹⁵⁄₆₄in x ¹⁵⁄₆₄in)

Work in continuous rounds, starting with a magic ring in Mid Brown.

Round 1: 10dc into ring (10 sts).

Round 2: 2dc in every st (20 sts).

Round 3: 1dc in every st.

Round 4: [Dc2tog, 3dc] 4 times (16 sts).

Round 5: [FLss, 1ch] in every st (16 ch, 16 ss).

Change to Fawn Brown.

Round 6: BLss in any st in round 4, 1ch, 1BLdc in every st, ss to join (16 sts).

Rounds 7 to 9: Working in continuous rounds, 1dc in every st.

Round 10: [Dc2tog, 2dc] 4 times (12 sts).

Start stuffing.

Round 11: [Dc2tog] 6 times (6 sts).

Fasten off. Add extra stuffing and sew to close.

Using Black, embroider eyes between rows 8 and 9 about 4 sts apart, sew a little 'V' shape between them for a little smile.

FAIRY COTTAGE

Materials

- 0.75mm-0.9mm (14/10 to 14/8 steel) crochet hook (0.9mm will produce slightly larger item)
- Gütermann top stitching thread in Ecru 169, Dusky Blue 112, Lilac 158, Purple 810, Green 235, White 111
- Embroidery needle

Finished Size

20mm x 18mm x 18mm (^{25}⁄₃₂in x ⁴⁵⁄₆₄in x ⁴⁵⁄₆₄in)

Body

Round 1: Using Ecru make a magic ring, 6dc into ring, ss to first st to join (6 sts).

Round 2: 1ch (does not count as a st throughout), 2dc in every st, ss to join (12 sts).

Round 3: 1ch, [2dc in next st, 1dc] 6 times, ss to join (18 sts).

Round 4: 1ch, 1BLdc in every st, ss to join.

Rounds 5 to 9: 1ch, 1dc in every st, ss to join.

Fasten off, sew in ends. Embroider doors using Lilac, frames using Purple and small bushes using Green. Stuff body.

Roof

Work in continuous rounds, starting with a magic ring in Dusky Blue.

Round 1: 6dc into ring (6 sts).

Round 2: 1dc in every st.

Round 3: [2dc in next st, 1dc] 3 times (9 sts).

Round 4: [2dc in next st, 2dc] 3 times (12 sts).

Round 5: [2dc in next st, 3dc] 3 times (15 sts).

Round 6: [2dc in next st, 4dc] 3 times (18 sts).

Embroider details such as extra windows here, using White and Purple, before joining.

Round 7: Continue with Dusky Blue, working into each st in round 6 of the roof and the FL of each st in round 9 of body of house at the same time to join, and stuffing as you go, work [2dc in next st, 1dc] 9 times (27 sts).

Round 8: [Ss, 1ch] in every st, ss to join (27 ch, 27 ss).

Fasten off, sew in ends.

FROGGIE

Materials

- 0.5mm-0.6mm (12 steel) crochet hook (0.6mm will produce slightly larger item)
- Gütermann hand quilting cotton in Sage Green 8816, Dusky Teal 7325, Black 5201
- Embroidery needle

Finished Size

12mm x 12mm x 8mm (¹⁵⁄₃₂in x ¹⁵⁄₃₂in x ⁵⁄₁₆in)

Body

Work in continuous rounds, starting with a magic ring in Sage Green.

Round 1: 8dc into ring (8 sts).

Round 2: 2dc in every st (16 sts).

Round 3: [2dc in next st, 1dc] (24 sts).

Rounds 4 to 7: 1dc in every st.

Round 8: [Dc2tog, 10dc] twice (22 sts).

Round 9: [Dc2tog, 9dc] twice (20 sts).

Round 10: [Dc2tog, 8dc] twice (18 sts).

Round 11: 1dc in every st.

Round 12: Ss, 1tr, 2tr in next st, 3ss, 2tr in next st, 1tr, 2ss, 1tr, 2tr in next st, 3ss, 2tr in next st, 1tr, ss (makes 4 semi-circle shapes for eyes).

Fasten off. Stuff the body, line up the front and back of eyes together and sew across to join, making 2 dome shapes. Embroider eyes in Black onto the dome shapes.

Tummy

Round 1: Using Dusky Teal, make a magic ring, 7dc into ring, pull ring closed, do not join round (7 sts).

Round 2: 1ch (does not count as a st throughout), turn, 2dc, 2htr in next 3 sts, 2dc (10 sts).

Round 3: 1ch, turn, 3dc, 2htr in next 4 sts, 3dc (14 sts).

Fasten off and sew to front of frog body.

Arms (make 2)

Row 1: 5PCIC (see Crochet Techniques).

Row 2: 1ch, turn, 1dc in every st.

Fasten off and sew each arm to the sides of frog. The hand of the frog should overlap the tummy.

OWL

Materials

- 0.5mm-0.6mm (12 steel) crochet hook (0.6mm will produce slightly larger item)
- Gütermann hand quilting cotton in Stone Grey 6506, Dusky Teal 7325, Mid Blue 5725, Dark Red 2833, Black 5201
- Embroidery needle

Finished Size

12mm x 12mm x 8mm (¹⁵⁄₃₂in x ¹⁵⁄₃₂in x ⁵⁄₁₆in)

Body

Work in continuous rounds, starting with a magic ring in Stone Grey.

Round 1: 8dc into ring (8 sts).

Round 2: 2dc in every st (16 sts).

Round 3: [2dc in next st, 1dc] (24 sts).

Rounds 4 to 7: 1dc in every st.

Round 8: [Dc2tog, 10dc] twice (22 sts).

Round 9: 1dc in every st.

Round 10: [Dc2tog, 9dc] twice (20 sts).

Round 11: 1dc in every st.

Round 12: [Dc2tog, 8dc] twice (18 sts).

Rounds 13 and 14: 1dc in every st.

Stuff body.

Joining and Ears

[Ss, 4ch, ss] in first st, hold both sides of last round together, [1ch, ss] in next 8 sts joining both sides, [ss, 4ch, ss] in last st, fasten off and sew in ends.

Tummy

Round 1 (RS): Using Mid Blue, make a magic ring, 8dc into ring, fasten off, pull ring enough to make a semi-circle (8 sts).

Round 2 (RS): Join Dark Red in the first st with RS facing, 2dc in every st (16 sts).

Round 3 (RS): Join Dusky Teal in the first st with RS facing, 2dc in first st, 14dc, 3dc in next st, 3dc across the base of the semi-circle, 1dc in first st of round 2, ss into first st of this round to join.

Fasten off, leaving a long end of Dusky Teal to sew to body.

If crocheting this pattern using DK yarn, leave an opening to turn the tummy into a little pocket for treats.

Wing (make 2)

Round 1 (WS): Using Mid Blue make a magic ring, [4ch, 2dtr, 4ch, ss] into ring.

Round 2 (RS): 2ch, turn, [2dc, 1htr] in first ch-4 sp, [2tr, 2ch picot, 1tr] in sp between 2 dtr, [1htr, 2dc] in next ch-4 sp, 2ch, ss in magic ring.

Use yarn ends to sew wings to owl's body. The tips of the wings should overlap the Dusky Teal sts of the tummy. Embroider little upside down V's for eyes in Black above tummy 2 sts apart. Embroider a small triangle in Dark Red for beak between the eyes.

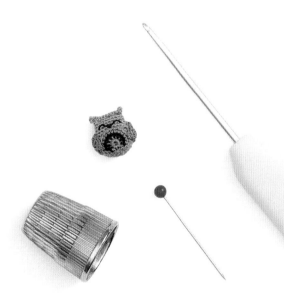

BUTTERFLY

Materials

- 0.5mm-0.6mm (12 steel) crochet hook (0.6mm will produce slightly larger item)
- 0.5mm wire and pliers (optional)
- Gütermann hand quilting cotton in Light Green 7918, Dusky Teal 7325, Dark Grey 5114, Light Pink 2538
- Embroidery needle

Finished Size

15mm x 15mm x 8mm (¹⁹⁄₃₂in x ¹⁹⁄₃₂in x ⁵⁄₁₆in)

Body

Work the body in continuous rounds, starting with a magic ring in Light Green.

Round 1: 8dc into ring (8 sts).

Round 2: 2dc in every st (16 sts).

Rounds 3 to 6: 1dc in every st.

Round 7: [Dc2tog, 2dc] 4 times (12 sts).

Rounds 8 and 9: 1dc in every st.

Stuff body.

Round 10: [Dc2tog] 6 times (6 sts).

Fasten off and sew body closed. Using Dark Grey embroider eyes between rounds 3 and 4, 3 sts apart and a little 'V' shape for the mouth. Using Light Pink add cheeks if required and small vertical stitches at outer edge of eyes.

Wire Antennae (optional)

Make a 'V' shape with wire and pliers, poke through magic ring or a stitch closer to the face and sew into place. Using Dark Grey, embroider eyes and a small smiley mouth. Add rosy cheeks using the light pink thread.

Wings

Using Dusky Teal make a magic ring.

Round 1 (RS): Into the ring work 2ch (counts as htr), 3htr, 2ch, 2htr, 2ch, 4htr, 2ch, 2htr, 2ch, ss in beg st to join (makes granny rectangle with 4 ch-2 sps).

Round 2 (WS): Turn, **[ss, 5ch, 5ttr, 5ch, ss] in same ch-2 sp**, 1ch, *[ss, 4ch, 4dtr, 4ch, ss] in next ch-2 sp*, 2ch, rep from * to * in next ch sp, 1ch, rep from ** to ** in last ch sp (makes 4 wings, bottom ones slightly smaller than top ones).

Round 3 (RS): Turn, **1ch, 5dc in ch-4 sp, 2dc between all ttr sts, 5dc in next ch-4 sp, 1ch, ss in ch-2 sp at base of wing in round 1**, 1ch, *ss in next ch-2 sp at base of wing from round 1, 1ch, 4dc in ch-4 sp, 1dc between all dtr sts, 4dc in next ch-4 sp, 1ch, ss in same ch-2 sp at base of wing from round 1*, 2ch, rep from * to * on next wing, 1ch, rep from ** to ** for last wing.

Fasten off. Position wings on back of body so that WS of rounds 1 and 2 make contact with body. Sew into place using yarn ends from round 1.

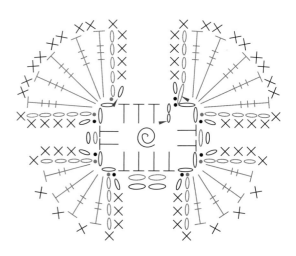

Butterfly Wings

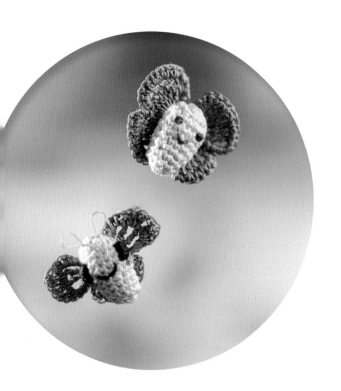

MOTH

Materials

- 0.5mm-0.6mm (12 steel) crochet hook (0.6mm will produce slightly larger item)
- 0.5mm wire and pliers (optional)
- Gütermann hand quilting cotton in Ivory 919, Fawn Brown 1225, Black 5201, Light Pink 2538
- Embroidery needle

Finished Size

13mm x 17mm x 8mm (3³⁄₆₄in x 4³⁄₆₄in x ⁵⁄₁₆in)

Body

Work as for butterfly body using Ivory. Using Black embroider larger eyes 5 sts apart, and a semi-circle for the mouth. Using Light Pink add cheeks if required. Add optional wire antennae as butterfly if you choose to.

Wings

Round 1 (RS): Using Ivory, make a magic ring, into ring work [5ch, 4dc, 3ch, ss in second ch of beg 5 ch] (4 sts, 2 ch-3 sps).

Change to Fawn Brown.

Round 2 (RS): [Ss, 5ch, 2ttr, 5ch, ss, 3ch, ss] in ch-3 sp, [ss, 3ch, ss, 5ch, 2ttr, 5ch, ss] in next ch-3 sp (makes top wings and 2 ch-3 sps for bottom wings).

Round 3 (WS): 1ch, turn, [5dc, 1htr] in ch-5 sp, 3tr between ttr sts, [2tr, 1htr, 4dc] in ch-5 sp, 1ch, [ss, 3ch, 3tr, 1dtr, 4ch, ss] in ch-3 sp, [ss, 4ch, 1dtr, 3tr, 3ch, ss] in next ch-3 sp, [1ch, 4dc, 1htr, 2tr] in ch-5 sp, 3tr between ttr sts, [1htr, 5dc, 1ch, ss] in ch-5 sp (reinforces top wings and adds bottom wings).

Fasten off and sew in Fawn Brown ends. Position wings on back of body so that WS of rounds 1 and 2 make contact with body. Sew into place using yarn ends from round 1.

LADYBIRD

Materials

- 0.5mm-0.6mm (12 steel) crochet hook (0.6mm will produce slightly larger item)
- Gütermann hand quilting cotton in Black 5201, Mid Red 2453, White 5709
- Embroidery needle

Finished Size

5mm x 7mm x 12mm (¹³⁄₆₄in x ⁹⁄₃₂in x ¹⁵⁄₃₂in)

Round 1: Using Mid Red, make a magic ring, 8dc into ring, ss to join (8 sts).

Round 2: 1ch, 2dc in every st, ss to join (16 sts).

Round 3: 1ch, 2dc in next st, 6dc, 2dc in next 2 sts, 6dc, 2dc in last st, ss to join and fasten off (20 sts).

Change to Black.

Round 4: BLss in first dc of round 3, 1BLdc in every st, join to first st with 1htr, [ch 4, 5BLdtr, 4ch, ss] in htr sp (20 sts, 1 bobble for head).

Round 5: [Dc2tog, 1dc] 6 times, dc2tog, ss first st to join (13 sts).

Stuff ladybird.

Round 6: [Dc2tog] 6 times, 1dc in last st, ss to join (7 sts).

Sew hole closed and fasten off. Leave long tail for additional sewing and embroidery.

Sew top of bobble onto body at round 2 to fully form the head and sew into place. Using Black, embroider a line to define the shell using the magic ring and the top of the head as a guide for symmetrical halves. Sew Black dots on the shell and White dots on either side of the head.

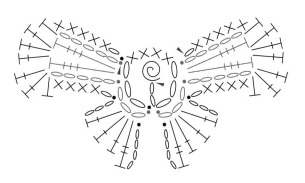

Moth Wings

About Town

For me, this chapter is reminiscent of childhood playtime. Characters from my favourite children's TV shows kept popping into my mind as I was designing the items. Few things are as nostalgic as a cheerful theme tune accompanying a familiar character in a brightly coloured town.

This chapter is a good introduction to crocheting geometric shapes, such as the house and café. Each piece can be adapted by customising the embroidered detailing, colourways, thread thicknesses and hook sizes to add variety to building types and sizes. By the time you have explored this chapter, you might end up with a whole street!

HOUSE

Materials

- 0.75mm-0.9mm (14/10 to 14/8 steel) crochet hook (0.9mm will produce slightly larger item)
- Gütermann top stitching thread in Dark Red/Brown 369, Light Brown 868, Bright Red 156, White 111, Green 235, Lilac 158, Dusty Pink 716
- Embroidery needle
- Cardboard for stiffening walls, base and roof

Finished Size

30mm x 20mm x 20mm (1³⁄₁₆in x ²⁵⁄₃₂in x ²⁵⁄₃₂in)

Walls

Using Light Brown make 41ch.

Row 1 (WS): Starting in second ch from hook, [1dc in each of next 10 ch, 1ch] 4 times (40 dc, 40 ch-1 sp).

Row 2: Turn, [1dc in each of next 10 dc, 1ch] 4 times.

Rows 3 to 10: Rep row 2.

Row 11: Turn, dc2tog, 6dc, dc2tog, leave rem sts unworked (8 sts).

Row 12: 1ch, turn, dc2tog, 4dc, dc2tog (6 sts).

Row 13: 1ch, turn, dc2tog, 2dc, dc2tog (4 sts).

Row 14: 1ch, turn, [dc2tog] twice (2 sts).

Row 15: 1ch, turn, dc2tog (1 st).

Fasten off. This is side D on diagram.

Skip next 10 dc sts and ch-1 sp (side C) from Row 10, repeat rows 11 to 15 over next set of 10 dc (side B). Fasten off.

Roof Panels (E and F)

Using Dark Red/Brown make 11ch.

Row 1: Starting in second ch from hook, 1dc in every st (10 sts).

Row 2: 1ch, turn, join to top of side wall C by working 1dc in every st of roof and BL of row 10 of wall together (10 sts).

Rows 3 to 7: 1ch, turn, 1dc in every st, fasten off, leave long tails for sewing.

Repeat for roof panel F, joining to top of side wall A in row 2.

Base (Panel G)

Row 1: Using Light Brown [ss, 1ch, 1dc] in first foundation ch from side panel A, 1dc in next 9 sts (10 sts).

Rows 2 to 10: 1ch, turn, 1dc in every st. Fasten off, leave long tails for sewing.

Embroider windows using White, top window frames and doors using Bright Red and bottom window frames using Dark Red/Brown. Add random Green stitches for foliage, then Dusky Pink and Lilac French knots for flowers.

Cut out pieces of cardboard, slightly smaller than each wall, base and roof panel and tack them to the inner sides. This keeps the sides flat when stuffing.

Stuff work and sew sides together using whipstitch. Join row 6 (last but one row of roof) in BL to row 10 of side wall A in BL only using ss.

Chimney

Using Dark Red/Brown make 2ch.

Rows 1 to 5: 1ch, turn, 1dc in every st.

Fold the top over so that there are 3 rows on one side and 2 on the other side. This makes a slant at the chimney base for sewing onto roof. Whipstitch up the sides and sew onto the roof, 2 sts in from the edge.

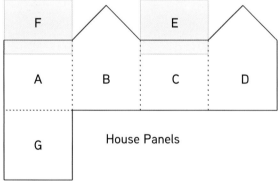

House Panels

CAFÉ

Materials

- 0.75mm-0.9mm (14/10 to 14/8 steel) crochet hook (0.9mm will produce slightly larger item)
- Gütermann top stitching thread in Light Pink 758, Bright Pink 382, Dusty Pink 716, Tan 982, Light Blue 143, White 111, Light Green 152
- Gütermann hand quilting cotton in White 5709, Brown 1833
- Embroidery needle
- Cardboard for stiffening walls and roof (optional)

Finished Size

20mm x 22mm x 15mm ($^{25}/_{32}$in x $^{55}/_{64}$in x $^{19}/_{32}$in)

Walls and Roof

Starting on panels A, B and C together (see diagram) using Light Pink, make 29ch.

Row 1: Starting in second ch from hook, 1dc in each of next 10 ch sts, 1ch, 1dc in each of next 8 sts, 1ch, 1dc in each of remaining 10 sts (28 sts, 2 ch sts).

Rows 2 to 14: 1ch, turn, 1dc in next 10 sts, 1ch, 1dc in next 8 sts, 1ch, 1dc in next 10 sts (28 sts, 2ch sts).

Fasten off, leaving a long tail for sewing.

Row 15 (RS): Turn, re-attach Light Pink into the first st in base panel B with a BLss, 1BLdc in same st, 1BLdc in remaining 7 sts of panel B (8 sts, start of panel D).

Rows 16 to 24: 1ch, turn, 1dc in next 8 sts.

Fasten off, leaving a long tail end for sewing. Change to Bright Pink.

Row 25 (RS): Turn, attach Bright Pink into first st with a BLss, 1BLdc in same st, 1BLdc in remaining 7 sts (8 sts, start of panel E).

Rows 26 to 38: 1ch, turn, 1dc in every st.

Fasten off, leaving a long tail end for sewing. Change back to Light Pink.

Row 39 (RS): turn, re-attach Light Pink into first st with a BLss, 1BLdc in same st, 1BLdc in remaining 7 sts (8 sts, start of panel F).

Rows 40 to 48: 1ch, turn, 1dc in every st.

Fasten off, leaving a long tail end for sewing.

Canopy

Using Bright Pink, make 6ch.

Row 1: [1htr, 1dc] in second ch from hook, [1htr, 1dc] in each rem ch (5 bobbles).

Fasten off, leaving long ends for sewing.

Sign

Using Dusty Pink, make 7ch.

Round 1: 1ch, turn, 1dc in every ch (6 sts).

Round 2: 1ch, turn, 2dc in first st, 4dc, 4dc in last st, continue to work on underside of sts, 4dc, 2dc in next st, ss to first st of round to join.

Fasten off, leaving a long tail end for sewing. Embroider the letters CAFE or any other lettering on the sign using White 5709.

Roof Topper

Using Bright Pink, make 3ch.

Row 1: Starting in second ch from hook, 1dc in every st (2 sts).

Rows 2 to 6: 1ch, turn, 1dc in every st.

Border: 1ch, turn, 1dc in next st, 3dc in next st (for corner), 1dc in next 4 sts down side of rectangle, 3dc in next 2 sts (for 2 corners), 1dc in next 4 sts up other side, 2dc in first st, ss to join.

Fasten off and sew to the top of panel E (roof) for extra height.

Using Light Blue sew the Canopy to the front and the shop sign to the top of the side panel above the canopy. Embroider doors, windows, lighting, plants and furniture around the walls using Light Blue, White 111, Light Green, Bright Pink, Dusky Pink, Tan and Brown.

Optional: cut out pieces of card slightly smaller than each panel.

Use the long tail ends to tack them to the underside of each panel to keep them flat. Sew panels together using whipstitch along the edges. Sew around the roof panel with Bright Pink, stuffing as you go.

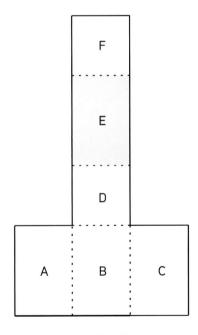

Café Panels

PUG THE POSTIE & LOLLIPOP LAPIN

Materials

0.5mm-0.6m (12 steel) crochet hook (0.6mm will produce slightly larger item)

- Gütermann hand quilting cotton in Light Brown 1225, Mid Red 2453, Dark Blue 5322, Grey/Blue 5815, Bright Pink 2955, Black 5201, Mustard 968 for Pug the Postie (PP); Yellow 758, Ivory 919, Orange 2045, Bright Pink 2955, Bright Red 1974, Black 5201, Light Grey 6506 for Lollipop Lapin (LL)
- 0.6mm wire and pliers
- Embroidery needle

Finished Size

13mm x 10mm x 10mm (³³⁄₆₄in x ²⁵⁄₆₄in x ²⁵⁄₆₄in)

Body

Work in continuous rounds, starting with a magic ring in Light Brown (PP) or Orange (LL).

Round 1: 8dc into ring (8 sts).

Round 2: 2dc in every st (16 sts).

Round 3: [2dc in next st, 1dc] 8 times, ss in next st to finish (24 sts).

Change to Mid Red (PP) or Yellow (LL), you will now join rounds.

Round 4: [BLss, 1ch, 1BLdc] in first st, BLdc in each rem st, ss to join (24 sts).

Rounds 5 to 7: 1ch, 1dc in every st, ss to join.

Change to Light Brown (PP) or Ivory (LL) and work in continuous rounds.

Round 8: [BLss, 1ch, 1BLdc] in first st, BLdc in each rem st (24 sts).

Round 9: [Dc2tog, 10dc] twice (22 sts).

Round 10: [Dc2tog, 9dc] twice (20 sts).

Stuff body.

Round 11: [Dc2tog] 10 times (10 sts).

Round 12: [Dc2tog] 5 times (5 sts).

Fasten off and sew to close hole.

Feet

Special stitches: 5dtrBO – 5 double treble st bobble (see Crochet Techniques)

Using Light Brown (PP) or Ivory (LL), [ss, 5dtrBO] in FL of the last dc on Round 3, fasten off. The seam from the Mid Red/Yellow rounds should be above and just to the left. This is going to be hidden with an arm later. Crochet second foot 6 sts to the right of first foot. Sew thread ends from top of bobble into base of bobble to give more folded shape.

Muzzle

Using Light Brown (PP) or Ivory (LL), make a magic ring.

Round 1: [3ch, 2tr, 1htr] into ring, change to Bright Pink, 3htr into ring, change to Light Brown, [1htr, 2tr, 3ch, ss] into ring, pull to close.

Sew to top half of body and between the feet, overlapping the last Mid Red/Yellow round slightly.

Top of Hat

Using Dark Blue (PP) or Yellow (LL) make a magic ring.

Round 1: 3ch (does not count as st), 15tr in ring, ss in first tr to join (15 sts).

Round 2: 1ch, 1dc in every st, ss to join.

Round 3: 1ch, [dc2tog, 3dc] 3 times, ss in first st to join (12 sts).

Fasten off.

Muzzle

Brim of Hat

Work in continuous rounds, starting with a magic ring in Dark Blue (PP) or Yellow (LL).

Round 1: 2ch (does not count as st), 12htr in ring, ss to join (12 sts).

Round 2: 2ch, 1htr in first st, 2htr in next 2 sts, [1htr, 2ch] in next st, leave rem sts unworked (6 sts).

Fasten off.

Sew brim and top hat together then attach to top of head.

Arms

Special stitches: 4trBO - 4 treble st bobble (see Crochet Techniques)

The arms are best worked after muzzle has been attached for better positioning.

Using Mid Red (PP) or Yellow (LL), make arms in FLs of round 8 of body. Count 2 sts from either side of muzzle, in the FL of next st work (ss, 3ch, 4trBO).

Fasten off. Use the thread end of the top of the bobble to sew into the FL (base of the stitch just made), so that it folds and puffs out even further.

Pug the Postie Ears (make 2)

Using Light Brown make a magic ring, 3ch, 3dtr, 3ch, ss into magic ring.

Fasten off, pull to close and sew to head, tucked close to hat.

Messenger Bag

Using Grey/Blue, make 4ch.

Rows 1 to 3: 1ch, turn, 1dc in every st (4 sts).

8ch, fasten off and sew to other corner of bag to make handle. Sew in place over arm, covering seams from Mid Red rounds.

Lollipop Lapin Ears (make 2)

Using Ivory, make 6ch.

Starting in second ch from hook, 1dc in next 2 ch, 1htr in next 2 ch, 5tr in next ch, working along opposite side of ch, 1htr in next 2 ch, 1dc in next 2 ch (13 sts).

Fasten off and sew to either side of head and side of hat so that they flop over.

Lollipop Disc (make 2)

Using Yellow, make a magic ring.

Round 1: 3ch, 15tr into ring, ss first st to join.

Sew in ends and embroider a Black stripe on one of the discs.

Cut wire to a length that is 1cm (⅜in) taller than the overall height of your amigurumi and make a loop on one end using pliers. Sew loop to the back of 1 disc. Place other disc on top of loop so wire is sandwiched in the middle. Make sure RS of embroidery is facing outwards.

Using Bright Red, [ss, 1ch] into BLs of front and back discs, joining both together and making an edging.

Thread wire through one of the arms, bend base of wire and stick it into one of the stitches on side of body.

Embroidery for Pug the Postie

Embroider eyes on either side of the muzzle using either Dark Blue to match the hat or Black thread. Use a running stitch to add a jacket split down the centre of the Mid Red stripes and a tiny emblem in Mustard.

Embroidery for Lollipop Lapin

Embroider eyes on either side of muzzle using Black, add 2 stripes to the high-vis jacket in Light Grey using a running stitch.

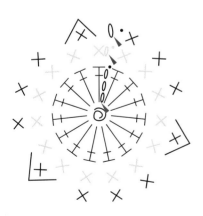

Top of hat

Brim of hat

POST BOX

Materials

- 0.75mm-0.9mm (14/10 to 14/8 steel) crochet hook (0.9mm will produce slightly larger item)
- Gütermann top stitching thread in Red 156, Black 000, White 111, Light Pink 758
- Embroidery needle
- 4mm-5mm (G6 to H8) crochet hook (to wrap the box around to make joining the box sides easier).

Finished Size

20mm x 9mm x 9mm ($^{25}\!/\!_{32}$in x $^{23}\!/\!_{64}$in x $^{23}\!/\!_{64}$in)

Box

This is worked as a flat panel.

Using Black make 10ch.

Rows 1 to 3: 1ch, turn, 1dc in every st (10 sts).

Change to Red.

Rows 4 to 11: 1ch, turn, 1dc in every st.

Fasten off. Embroider small White collection time sign in the centre of the rectangle and a Black slot above it. Using Black embroider eyes, 2 sts apart just above row 4 and a little 'V' between each one for the smile. Using Light Pink embroider cheeks.

Base

Round 1: Using Black make a magic ring, 12dc into ring, ss to join (12 sts).

Round 2: [1ch, ss] in every st. Fasten off, leaving a long tail for sewing (12 ss, 12 ch).

Top

Work in continuous rounds, starting with a magic ring in Red.

Round 1: 6dc into ring (6 sts).

Round 2: 2dc in every st (12 sts).

Round 3: [1ch, FLss] in every st, ss to join, leaving a long tail for sewing (12 ss, 12 ch).

Wrap box RS facing outwards around a 4mm-5mm (G6 to H8) crochet hook to help with this step. Sew the ends together to create a closed cylinder with the Black stripe at the bottom.

Whipstitch the ch sts of row 1 of the base together and pull to close. Sew ch sts from the base to round 1 of box. This gives a crisp and more solid edge to the cylinder shape.

Stuff work. Sew the BLs from round 2 of the top to the cylinder.

TRAFFIC LIGHT

Materials

- 0.75mm-0.9mm (14/10 to 14/8 steel) crochet hook (0.9mm will produce slightly larger item)
- Gütermann top stitching thread in Black 000; Gütermann hand quilting thread in Red 1974, Yellow 758, Emerald 8244
- Embroidery needle
- 0.6mm wire and pliers

Don't fancy crocheting in Black? Try a Mid Grey 701 instead, much easier on the eyes.

Finished Size

22mm x 5mm x 5mm ($^{55}\!/\!_{64}$in x $^{13}\!/\!_{64}$ x $^{13}\!/\!_{64}$in)

Traffic Light

Using Black, make 14ch.

Rows 1 and 2: 1ch, turn, 14dc (14 sts).

Fasten off leaving a long tail for sewing. Embroider traffic light circles to the lower half of the strip using Red, Yellow and Emerald.

Base

Round 1 (RS): Using Black make a magic ring, 9dc into ring, ss to join (9 sts).

Round 2: [1ch, ss] in every st (9 ch, 9 ss).

Fasten off leaving one long tail for sewing, weave in the other end.

Cut a length of wire approx 3cm (1⅛in) long and make a loop on one end just smaller than the crocheted base using pliers. Bend the rest of the wire so that it stands up straight from the centre of the wire loop. Thread the wire through the magic ring RS facing upwards. Sew the wire loop around the edge of the base on the underside.

Using pliers, make another loop narrower than the crocheted strip for the lights. Sew loop to one half of the strip. Fold strip in half and sew up the sides using whipstitch.

TREE

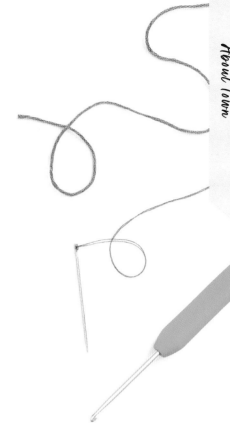

Materials

- 0.75mm-0.9mm (14/10 to 14/8 steel) crochet hook (0.9mm will produce slightly larger item)
- Gütermann top stitching thread in Dark Red/Brown 369, Emerald 237, Bright Red 156, Black 000, Light Pink 758
- Small button
- Embroidery needle

Finished Size

30mm x 20mm x 20mm (1³⁄₁₆in x ²⁵⁄₃₂in x ²⁵⁄₃₂in)

Special stitches: 5dtrpc - 5 double treble popcorn stitch:

- Make 5 double treble crochet stitches.
- Remove your hook from the last stitch and insert it between the first dtr and the stitch before it.
- Pull the loop from the last stitch through that stitch space. Ch 1 to close the Popcorn.

Round 1: Using Dark Red/Brown, make a magic ring, 10dc into ring, ss to join (10 sts).

Round 2: 1ch, [1dc, 2dc in next st] 5 times, ss to join (15 sts).

Crochet the rest of the tree in continuous rounds without joining.

Round 3: 1ch, BLdc in every st.

Rounds 4 to 6: 1dc in every st.

Stuff work, add a small button to the inside of the base to help keep flat when standing.

Round 7: [1dc, dc2tog] 5 times (10 sts).

Rounds 8 and 9: 1dc in every st, ss in next st to fasten off.

Change to Emerald.

Round 10: Ss in any st to join, 1ch, 2dc in every st, ss to join (20 sts).

Round 11: 1ch, 2dc in every st, ss to join (40 sts).

Stuff the tree trunk firmly.

Round 12: 2ch (counts as 1htr throughout), [5dtrpc in next st, 3htr] 9 times, 5dtrpc in next st, 2htr, ss in first 2ch to join (10 pc, 30 htr).

Round 13: 2ch, [skip pc, 3htr] 9 times, skip pc, 2htr, ss in 2ch to join (30 sts).

Round 14: 2ch, [5dtrpc in next st, 2htr] 9 times, 5dtrpc in next st, 1htr, ss in first 2ch to join (10 pc, 20 htr).

Round 15: 2ch, [skip pc, 2htr] 9 times, skip pc, 1htr, ss in 2ch to join (20 sts).

Round 16: 2ch, [5dtrpc in next st, 1htr] 9 times, 5dtrpc in next st, ss in first 2ch to join (10 pc, 10 htr).

Stuff the tree.

Round 17: 2ch, [skip pc, 1htr] 9 times, skip pc, ss in 2ch to join (10 sts).

Round 18: 2ch, [5dtrpc in next st, 1htr] 4 times, 5dtrpc in next st, ss in first 2ch to join (5pc, 5htr).

Ensure the tree is fully stuffed.

Round 19: 3ch, 5dtrpc in next st, fasten off and sew the last pc to finish top of tree by covering rem hole.

Round 20 (optional): Using Dark Red/Brown, [ss, 1ch] in every FL from round 3.

Embroider apples to pc sts and between pc sts of tree using Bright Red.

Embroider eyes between rounds 5 and 6 using Black, 6 sts apart. Embroider cheeks using Light Pink.

LITTLE CAR

Materials

- 0.75mm-0.9mm (14/10 to 14/8 steel) crochet hook (0.9mm will produce slightly larger item)
- Gütermann top stitching thread in Yellow 106, Light Blue 143, Ivory 414, White 111, Brown 369, Grey 701
- Embroidery needle

Finished Size

13mm x 14mm x 18mm (³³⁄₆₄in x ³⁵⁄₆₄in x ⁴⁵⁄₆₄in)

Car

Round 1: Using Light Blue, make a magic ring, 1ch, 6dc into ring, ss in first st to join (6 sts).

Round 2: 1ch, 2dc in first st, 1dc, 3dc in each of next 2 sts, 1dc, 3dc in next st, 1dc in first st, ss in next st to join (14 sts).

Round 3: 1ch, 1dc in first 4 sts, 2dc next st, 2dc, 2dc in next st, 3dc, 2dc in next st, 2dc, 1dc in first st, ss in next st to join (18 sts).

Change to Ivory.

Round 4: BLss in first st, 1BLdc in same st, 1BLdc in each rem st, ss to join (18 sts).

Round 5: 1ch, 1dc in same st, *3dc, 2dc in next st, 4dc, 2dc in next st, 3dc, 2dc in next st, 4dc, 1dc in beg round 4 st*, do not ss to join (22 sts).

Round 6: 1dc in every st, mark at 17th st, ss in first st of round to fasten off (22 sts).

Change to Light Blue.

Row 7: Start bonnet at marked st (17th st of round 6, top right corner), (ss, 1dc) in same st and next 5 sts (6 sts).

Rows 8 and 9: 1ch, turn, 1dc in each of the 6 sts (6 sts).

Round 10: Continue to body; 2dc down left side of bonnet, 5dc in sts from round 6, 2dc in next st, 4dc, 2dc in next st, 5dc, 2dc of right side of bonnet, 1BLdc in 6 sts of row 9 (28 sts).

Rounds 11 and 12: 1dc in every st (28 sts).

Work base of car in rows.

Row 1: 1ch, turn, 1FLdc in next 6 sts (6 sts).

Rows 2 to 7: 1ch, turn, 1dc in every st (6 sts).

Row 8: 1ch, turn, dc2tog, 2dc, dc2tog (4 sts).

Fasten off. Sew the base panel to the BLs of round 12, stuff before sewing completely closed.

Wheels (make 4)

Round 1: Using Brown, make a magic ring, 6dc into ring, fasten off and make an invisible ss to join to the first st (see Crochet Techniques) (6 sts).

Change to Light Blue for wheel arches.

Round 2: Ss in any round 1 st, 1dc in same st, 3dc in next 2 sts, 1dc, 1ch, ss in same st as last dc worked, fasten off and use Light Blue tails to sew onto sides of the car.

Embroider Light Blue lines connecting the corners of the Light Blue roof to the corners of body of car as partitions for the windows. Embroider headlights in Yellow, licence plates in White and windscreen wipers in Grey for extra detail.

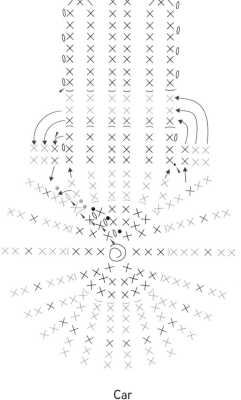

Car

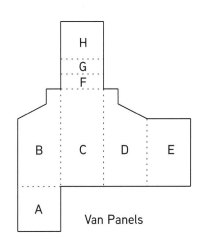

TRAFFIC CONE

Materials

- 0.5mm-0.6mm (12 steel) crochet hook (0.6mm will produce slightly larger item)
- Gütermann hand quilting cotton in Orange 2045, Ivory 919, Black 5201
- Embroidery needle

Finished Size

10mm x 7mm x 7mm (²⁵⁄₆₄in x ⁹⁄₃₂in x ⁹⁄₃₂in)

Cone

Work in continuous rounds, starting with a magic ring in Orange.

Round 1: 8dc into ring (8 sts).

Round 2: [2dc in next st, 3dc] twice (10 sts).

Rounds 3 to 5: 1dc in every st.

Round 6: [2dc in next st, 4dc] twice (12 sts).

Rounds 7 to 9: 1dc in every st.

Round 10: [3FLdc in first st, 2dc] 4 times (16 sts).

Fasten off, leaving a long tail for sewing.

Base

Round 1 (RS): Using Orange make a magic ring, 2ch (does not count as htr), 12htr into ring, ss to join (12 sts).

Round 2: 1ch, [3dc in first st, 2dc] 4 times (16 sts).

Fasten off and sew in ends.

Stuff cone shape. Join base to the cone. Align the corners and whipstitch BLs together.

Embroider stripes in Ivory and eyes and mouth in Black.

LITTLE VAN

Materials

- 0.75mm-0.9mm (14/10 to 14/8 steel) crochet hook (0.9mm will produce slightly larger item)
- Gütermann top stitching thread in Red 156, White 111, Black 000, Yellow 106
- Embroidery needle
- Cardboard for stiffening van panels

Finished Size

13mm x 13mm x 15mm (³³⁄₆₄in x ³³⁄₆₄in x ¹⁹⁄₃₂in)

Using Red, make 7ch.

Panel A

Row 1 (RS): Starting in second ch from hook, 1dc in every st (6 sts).

Rows 2 to 5: 1ch, turn, 1dc in every st.

Panels B, C, D and E

Row 6: 1ch, turn, 1dc in every st, make 19ch.

Row 7: Starting in second ch from hook, [1dc next 6 sts, 1ch] 3 times, 1BLdc in rem 6 sts (24 dc, 3 ch-1 sp).

Rows 8 to 15: 1ch, turn, [1dc in next 6 sts, 1ch] 3 times, 1 dc in next 6 sts (24 dc, 3 ch-1 sp).

Row 16: 1ch, turn, dc2tog, 4dc, 1ch, 6dc, 1ch, 4dc, dc2tog, leave rem sts unworked (16 dc, 2 ch-1 sp).

Row 17: 1ch, turn, dc2tog, 3dc, 1ch, 6dc, 1ch, 3dc, dc2tog (14 dc, 2 ch-1 sp).

Row 18: 1ch, turn, dc2tog, 2dc, 1ch, 6dc, 1ch, 2dc, dc2tog (12 dc, 2 ch-1 sp).

Row 19: 1ch, turn, dc2tog, 1dc, 1ch, 6dc, 1ch, 1dc, dc2tog (10 dc, 2 ch-1 sp).

Row 20: 1ch, turn, 2dc, 1ch, 6dc, 1ch, 2dc (10 sts, 2 ch-1 sp).

Fasten off.

Panel F

Row 21 (RS): Turn, attach Red with a BLss in first dc of Panel C, [1ch, 1BLdc] in same st, 1BLdc in next 5 sts, leave rem sts unworked (6 sts).

Row 22: 1ch, turn, 1dc in every st.

Panel G

Row 23: 1ch, turn, 1BLdc in every st (6 sts).

Row 24: 1ch, turn, 1dc in every st, fasten off.

Panel H

Row 25 (RS): Turn, attach White with a BLss in first dc of Panel G, [1ch, 1BLdc] in same st, 1BLdc in next 5 sts (6 sts).

Row 26: 1ch, turn, 1dc in every st.

Row 27 (RS): Turn, attach Red with a BLss in first st, [1ch, 1BLdc] in same st, 1BLdc in next 5 sts (6 sts).

Rows 28 to 30: 1ch, turn, 1dc in every st, fasten off and sew in ends.

All unworked loops from the rows worked in BL (rows 7, 21, 23, 25 and 27) should be on RS of work.

Embroider detailing such as doors, windows, bumper and licence plates onto this side, using White and Black.

Tack cardboard squares to WS to keep panels flat when stuffing.

Sew up sides using whipstitch, stuffing as you go. Embroider headlights in Yellow.

Wheels (make 4)

Using Black make a magic ring, 8dc into ring, pull to close, fasten off and make an invisible ss to join to the first st (see Crochet Techniques) to finish round. Use tail ends to sew wheels to van.

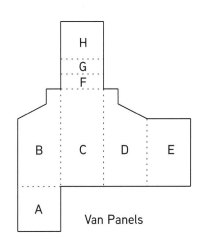

Van Panels

Fruit & Veg

Get your dose of vitamin C with these tiny bright and colourful friends! These are a great introduction to micro amigurumi as you can explore how simple shapes are made, you can also swap colours to widen the variety of fruit & veg. Turn the beetroot into a parsnip or garlic by crocheting in white thread or give that pear a purple make-over so it becomes a happy little aubergine. Don't forget that you can size up your hook and thread, then work your way down to super tiny when you feel ready. The pieces in this chapter are made with Gütermann top stitching thread and hand quilting cotton, and a 0.75mm (14/10 steel) hook.

BANANA

Materials

- 0.75mm (14/10 steel) crochet hook
- Gütermann top stitching thread in Yellow 106, Dark Red 369; Gütermann hand quilting cotton in Black 5201
- Embroidery needle

Finished Size

20mm x 15mm x 6mm (²⁵⁄₃₂in x ¹⁹⁄₃₂in x ¹⁵⁄₆₄in)

Using Yellow make 18ch.

Row 1 (WS): Starting in second ch from hook, 17dc (17 sts).

Row 2: 1ch, turn, 2BLss, 2BLdc, [1BLhtr, 2BLhtr in next st] 4 times, 1BLhtr, 2BLdc, 2BLss (21 sts).

Row 3: 1ch, turn, 2FLss, 17FLdc, 2FLss.

Row 4: 1ch, turn, 2BLss, 2BLdc, 13BLhtr, 2BLdc, 2BLss.

Row 5: Rep row 3.

Row 6: 1ch, turn, 2BLss, 2BLdc, [1BLhtr, BLhtr2tog] 4 times, 1BLhtr, 2BLdc, 2BLss (17 sts).

Row 7: 1ch, turn, 2FLss, 13FLdc, 2FLss.

Fasten off leaving a long end for sewing. Embroider face using Black on the RS of banana.

Use whipstitch to sew first ch row to BL of row 7. This joins the sides and creates inner curve of banana. Stuff banana as you sew and close the ends. Add further embroidery to the ends using Dark Red.

STRAWBERRY

Materials

- 0.75mm (14/10) crochet hook
- Gütermann top stitching thread in Green 235, Red 156; Gütermann hand quilting cotton in Black 5201
- Embroidery needle

Finished Size

15mm x 9mm x 9mm (¹⁹⁄₃₂in x ²³⁄₆₄in x ²³⁄₆₄in)

Body

Work in continuous rounds, starting with a magic ring in Red.

Round 1: 6dc into ring (6 sts).

Round 2: [2dc in next st, 2dc] twice (8 sts).

Round 3: [2dc in next st, 3dc] twice (10 sts).

Round 4: [2dc in next st, 4dc] twice (12 sts).

Round 5: [2dc in next st, 5dc] twice (14 sts).

Stuff strawberry.

Round 6: [Dc2tog] 7 times (7 sts).

Fasten off and sew hole to close.

Stalk

Using Green, make 4PCIC (see Crochet Techniques), *4ch, ss in third ch from hook, rep from * 2 to 4 more times. Fasten off.

Sew stalk to top of strawberry. Embroider eyes between rounds 4 and 5 in Black 4 sts apart. Embroider mouth in the 4 sts between eyes using Black.

PEAR

Materials

- 0.75mm (14/10) crochet hook
- Gütermann top stitching thread in Light Green 152, Dark Red 369; Gütermann hand quilting cotton in Black 5201
- Embroidery needle

Finished Size

19mm x 10mm x 10mm (¾in x ²⁵⁄₆₄in x ²⁵⁄₆₄in)

Stalk

Row 1: Using Dark Red make 4ch, fasten off.

Body

Work in continuous rounds, starting with a magic ring in Light Green.

Round 1: 8dc into ring (8 sts).

Round 2: 2dc in every st (16 sts).

Rounds 3 to 5: 1dc in every st.

Round 6: [2dc, dc2tog] 4 times (12 sts).

Stuff pear, continue to stuff as you crochet further rounds.

Round 7: [2dc, dc2tog] 3 times (9 sts).

Round 8: 1dc in every st.

Fasten off.

Place stalk in opening of round 8 with the tail ends inside. Sew the opening closed using Light Green, trapping the stalk. Embroider eyes between rounds 4 and 5 using Black, 5 sts apart. Embroider mouth below eyes on row 4 using Black.

CARROT

Materials

- 0.75mm (14/10) crochet hook
- Gütermann top stitching thread in Orange 364, Green 235; Gütermann hand quilting cotton in Black 5201, Pale Pink 2538
- Embroidery needle

Finished Size

19mm x 7mm x 5mm (¾in x ⁹⁄₃₂in x ¹³⁄₆₄in)

Body

Work in continuous rounds, starting with a magic ring in Orange.

Round 1: 6dc into ring (6 sts).

Round 2: [2dc, 2dc in next st] twice (8 sts).

Round 3: 1dc in every st.

Round 4: [3dc, 2dc in next st] twice (10 sts).

Rounds 5 to 7: 1dc in every st.

Stuff carrot.

Round 8: [Dc2tog] 5 times (5 sts).

Fasten off leaving a long tail.

Stalk

Using Green, make 6ch, ss in first ch, [6 ch, ss in same ch] twice (3 loops).

Fasten off leaving a long tail for sewing. Embroider eyes between rounds 5 and 6, 2 sts apart in Black. Add cheeks in Pale Pink if desired and a mouth in Black on row 5.

Insert the connected end of the stalk into the small opening at top of carrot. Use a long Orange thread tail to sew the hole closed, trapping the stalk end.

BROCCOLI

Materials

- 0.75mm (14/10) crochet hook
- Gütermann top stitching thread in Green 235, Light Green 152; Gütermann hand quilting cotton in Black 5201
- Embroidery needle

Finished Size

19mm x 15mm x 15mm (¾in x ¹⁹⁄₃₂in x ¹⁹⁄₃₂in)

Special stitches: pc st - popcorn st made with 5 tr sts:

- Make 5 treble crochet stitches.
- Remove your hook from the last stitch and insert it between the first tr and the stitch before it.
- Pull the loop from the last stitch through that stitch space. Ch 1 to close the Popcorn.

Work in continuous rounds, starting with a magic ring in Light Green.

Round 1: 8dc into ring (8 sts).

Round 2: 1BLdc in every st.

Rounds 3 and 4: 1dc in every st.

Round 5: [2dc in next st, 3dc] twice (10 sts).

Fasten off.

Round 6: Join Green with a ss in FL of any st, [3ch, 4tr] in first st to make first pc, 1ch, [1 pc, 1ch] in each rem st, ss in beg 3ch to join (10 pc, 10 ch-1 sp).

Round 7: 3ch, 1pc in every ch sp, ss in beg pc to finish (10 pc).

Stuff the broccoli. Cut yarn leaving an end long enough to make 1 bobble st, sew closed to last st, work [ss, 3ch, 5trtog] in last st, fasten off. Sew top of bobble onto top of broccoli head, covering any gap.

Using black thread, sew eyes and a little smile onto the broccoli stalk.

PEPPER

Materials

- 0.75mm (14/10) crochet hook
- Gütermann top stitching thread in Green 235, Red 156; Gütermann hand quilting cotton in Black 5201
- Embroidery needle

Finished Size

12mm x 12mm x 12mm ($^{15}/_{32}$in x $^{15}/_{32}$in x $^{15}/_{32}$in)

Stalk

Using Green, ch3, fasten off, leaving a tail for sewing.

Body

Work in continuous rounds, starting with a magic ring in Red.

Round 1: 6dc into ring (6 sts).

Round 2: 2dc in every st (12 sts).

Round 3: [3dc in first st, 2dc] 4 times (20 sts).

Rounds 4 and 5: 1dc in every st.

Round 6: [Dc2tog, 3dc] 4 times (16 sts).

Stuff pepper, continue to stuff as you crochet further rounds.

Round 7: 1dc in every st, repeat row for a longer pepper (12 sts).

Round 8: [Dc2tog, 2dc] 4 times (12 sts).

Round 9: [Dc2tog] 6 times (6 sts).

Lightly stuff pepper, it needs to be roomy inside for sewing up.

Fasten off and sew to close. Wrap the thread lightly around the pepper and through the centre of the pepper 4 times. This creates the segments, the tighter the wraps the shorter and more pronounced the segments will be.

Sew stalk to top of pepper.

Embroider eyes on round 5 of pepper using Black approx 3-4 sts apart. Embroider mouth using Black over top of wrapped threads just below the eyes.

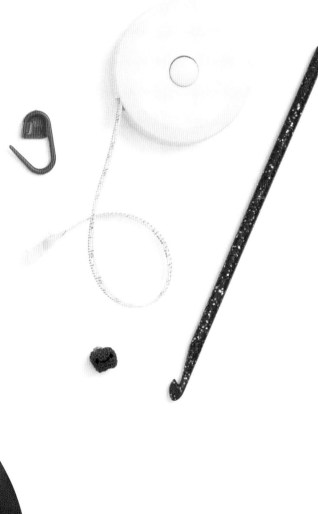

BEETROOT

Materials

- 0.75mm (14/10) crochet hook
- Gütermann top stitching thread in Green 235, Red 46; Gütermann hand quilting cotton in Black 5201
- Embroidery needle

Finished Size

25mm x 11mm x 11mm (63/64in x 7/16in x 7/16in)

Leaves (make 3)

Using Green make 4ch, starting in second ch from hook, 1dc in next 2 ch, 6dc in last ch, working on opposite side of ch, 1dc in next ch, ss onto next ch, 3ch (or more for longer stalks), fasten off leaving a long tail for sewing.

Body

Work in continuous rounds, starting with a magic ring in Red.

Round 1: 6dc into ring (6 sts).

Round 2: 2dc in every st (12 sts).

Round 3: [2dc, 2dc in next st] 4 times (16 sts).

Rounds 4 and 5: 1dc in every st.

Round 6: [2dc, dc2tog] 4 times (12 sts).

Sew the long ends of the leaves through the magic ring and secure inside. Stuff the beetroot.

Round 7: [Dc2tog] 6 times (6 sts).

Round 8: [Dc2tog] 3 times, 3ch (3 dc, 3 ch).

Fasten off, leaving a length of tail for root strands.

Embroider face between rounds 4 to 5 using Black, spacing the eyes 4 sts apart. Embroider mouth in the 4 sts between eyes using Black.

BEAN

Materials

- 0.75mm (14/10) crochet hook
- Gütermann top stitching thread in Beige 722; Gütermann hand quilting cotton in Black 5201
- Embroidery needle

Finished Size

18mm x 12mm x 8mm (45/64in x 15/32in x 5/16in)

Work in continuous rounds, starting with a magic ring in Beige.

Round 1: 6dc into ring (6 sts).

Round 2: 2dc in every st (12 sts).

Round 3: 4dc, 2dc in next 4 sts, 4dc (16 sts).

Rounds 4 and 5: [Dc2tog] twice, 3dc, 2dc in next 3 sts, 4dc, dc2tog (16 sts).

Rounds 6 to 8: 2dc in next 2 sts, 3dc, [dc2tog] 3 times, 4dc, 2dc in last st (16 sts).

Stuff bean, continue to stuff as you crochet further rounds.

Round 9: 2dc in first st, [dc2tog] 3 times, 2dc, [dc2tog] 3 times, 2dc in last st (12 sts).

Round 10: [Dc2tog] 6 times (6 sts).

Fasten off and sew end to close. Embroider eyes 4 sts apart using Black between rounds 7 and 8. Embroider mouth on row below between eyes using Black.

SPROUT

Materials

- 0.75mm (14/10) crochet hook
- Gütermann top stitching thread in Light Green 152; Gütermann hand quilting cotton in Black 5201, Pink 3526
- Embroidery needle

Finished Size

12mm x 12mm x 12mm (¹⁵⁄₃₂in x ¹⁵⁄₃₂in x ¹⁵⁄₃₂in)

Body

Work in continuous rounds, starting with a magic ring in Light Green.

Round 1: 6dc into ring [6 sts].

Round 2: 2dc in every st (12 sts).

Round 3: [2dc in next st, 1dc] 6 times (18 sts).

Rounds 4 and 5: 1dc in every st.

Round 6: [Dc2tog, 1dc] 6 times (12 sts).

Stuff sprout.

Round 7: [Dc2tog] 6 times (6 sts).

Fasten off, stuff and sew in ends.

Leaves (make 4)

Rounds 1 to 3: Rep rounds 1 to 3 of body.

Round 4: 2dc in next 4 sts, ss in next 2 sts, leave rem sts unworked (8 dc, 2 ss).

Fasten off, leaving long tails for sewing. Makes 'petal' shape with slightly curled edge.

Position leaves onto body so that they form an overlapped diamond shape. The curled edge of round 4 should surround the side where you want the face to be. Use thread ends to sew them in place, ensuring that they overlap each other slightly.

Eyes should be embroidered near the 'corners' of the diamond shape, 2 sts apart, using Black. Add cheeks in Pink and mouth and eyelashes in Black if desired.

AVOCADO

Materials

- 0.75mm (14/10) crochet hook
- Gütermann top stitching thread in Green 235, Light Green 152 and Dark Red 369; Gütermann hand quilting cotton in Black 5201 and Pink 3526
- Embroidery needle

Finished Size

14mm x 12mm x 7mm (³⁵⁄₆₄in x ¹⁵⁄₃₂in x ⁹⁄₃₂in)

Face

Round 1: Using Dark Red make a magic ring, 8dc into ring, ss to join (8 sts).

Change to Light Green.

Round 2: [Ss, 1ch, 2dc] in first st, 2dc in next 5 sts, [1htr, 2tr] in next st, [2tr, 1htr] in next st, ss to first dc to join (18 sts).

Round 3: 1dc in next 14 sts, [1dc, 1htr] in next st, [1htr, 1dc] in next st, 1dc in last 2 sts (20 sts).

Fasten off and sew in ends.

Outer Skin

Using Green make a magic ring.

Rounds 1 to 3: Rep rounds 1 to 3 of face with no colour changes (20 sts).

Rounds 4 and 5: 1dc in every st.

Fasten off and sew in ends. Embroider face just above the avocado stone between rounds 2 and 3 using Black for the eyes and nose, and Pink for the cheeks. Stuff outer skin, attach face by sewing the BLs of the last rounds together using Green, working 2 whipstitches per crochet st to frame the face nicely.

Food

These tiny morsels of goodness will certainly sort out your grumbly tummy. Reminiscent of childhood parties and trips to the cinema, these snacks would make excellent jewellery or charm accessories. Some are super simple while others require some embroidery detailing. Team with ami from the Fruit & Veg chapter for a more balanced meal, or the Back to School chapter to get your packed lunch ready!

They have been crocheted with Gütermann top stitching thread and a 0.75mm (14/10 steel) hook, but don't forget that you can size up your thread and hook if you require bigger portions!

BIRTHDAY CAKE

Materials

- 0.75mm-0.9mm (14/10 to 14/8 steel) crochet hook (0.9mm will produce slightly larger item)
- Gütermann top stitching thread in Bright Pink 382, Ivory 414, Light Pink 758, Yellow 106, Black 000, White 111
- Embroidery needle

Finished Size

24mm x 22mm x 22mm (15⁄16in x 55⁄64in x 55⁄64in)

Cake Base

Round 1: Using Ivory, make a magic ring, 6dc into ring, ss to first st to join (6 sts).

Round 2: 1ch (does not count as a st throughout), 2dc in every st, ss to join (12 sts).

Round 3: 1ch, [2dc in next st, 1dc] 6 times, ss to join (18 sts).

Round 4: 1ch, 1BLdc in every st, ss to join (18 sts).

Round 5: 1ch, 1dc in every st, ss to join.

Change to Bright Pink.

Round 6: [1BLss, 1BLdc] in first st, 1BLdc in every st, ss to join (18 sts).

Change to Ivory.

Rounds 7 and 8: As rounds 4 and 5, fasten off.

Embroider eyes using Black on round 4, 4 sts apart, add cheeks in Light Pink and mouth in Black if required.

Cake Top

Round 1: Using Light Pink, make a magic ring, 6dc into ring, ss to first st to join (6 sts).

Round 2: 1ch (does not count as a st throughout), 2dc in every st, ss to join (12 sts).

Round 3: 1ch, [2dc in next st, change to Bright Pink, 1dc in next st, change to Light Pink] 6 times, ss to first Light Pink st to join (18 sts, 12 Light Pink, 6 Bright Pink).

Fasten off and sew in ends.

Candle

Round 1: Using Yellow, make a magic ring, (2ch, 1tr, 2ch picot, 2ch, ss) in ring, fasten off.

Thread White strand though magic ring, make 6 or more forward knots (see Crochet Techniques) in White, trapping all 3 threads including the Yellow thread ends from the flame. Thread all ends through magic ring of cake top and sew to secure. Fasten off and stuff cake. Whipstitch BLs of cake top round 3 to FLs of cake base round 8.

SWEETIE

Materials

- 0.75mm-0.9mm (14/10 to 14/8 steel) crochet hook (0.9mm will produce slightly larger item)
- Gütermann top stitching thread in Light Green 152, Black 000, Bright Pink 382, Light Pink 758
- Embroidery needle

Finished Size

8mm x 22mm x 8mm (5⁄16in x 55⁄64in x 5⁄16in)

Wrapper Ends (make 2)

Work in continuous rounds, starting with a magic ring in Light Green.

Round 1: 8dc into ring (8 sts).

Round 2: [2dc in next st, 3dc] twice (10 sts).

Round 3: (Ss, 2ch) in every st (10 frills sts).

Body

Work in continuous rounds, starting with a magic ring in Light Green.

Round 1: 6dc into ring (6 sts).

Round 2: 2dc in every st (12 sts).

Round 3: [2dc in next st, 3dc] 3 times (15 sts).

Rounds 4 to 6: 1dc in every st.

Round 7: [Dc2tog, 3dc] 3 times (12 sts).

Stuff body.

Round 8: [Dc2tog] 6 times (6 sts).

Fasten off and sew closed. Sew wrapper ends to first and last round of body. Wrap Bright Pink thread around the joins and sew into place. Add 2 French knots in Black, 5 rounds apart for the eyes. Add a smile in Black and cheeks in Light Pink if required.

POPCORN

Materials

- 0.75mm-0.9mm (14/10 to 14/8 steel) crochet hook (0.9mm will produce slightly larger item)
- Gütermann top stitching thread in Red 156, Butter Brown 893, White 111, Black 000
- Embroidery needle

Finished Size

20mm x 15mm x 15mm ($^{25}\!/_{32}$in x $^{19}\!/_{32}$in x $^{19}\!/_{32}$in)

Box

Using Red, make 13ch.

Row 1 (RS): Starting in third ch from hook, 3htr, 4dc, 1ch (makes a 'foldable' edge), 4dc (11 sts, 1 ch).

Row 2: 1ch (does not count as a st throughout), turn, 4dc, 1ch, 4dc, 3htr.

Row 3: 2ch (does not count as a st throughout), turn, 3htr, 4dc, 1ch, 4dc.

Row 4: As row 2 (makes 1 side and 1 base).

Row 5: 2ch, turn, 3BLhtr, 4BLdc (makes edge of box).

Row 6: 1ch, turn, 4dc, 3htr.

Row 7: 2ch, turn, 3htr, 4dc.

Row 8: As row 6.

Repeat rows 5 to 8 twice more to make 2 more sides of box. Fasten off, leave long end for sewing.

Join Red at the bottom of the turning ch from row 1, [1ch, 6dc] on each of the 4 sides of box. Fasten off, leave long ends for sewing.

Using White, work either an embroidered running stitch or surface crochet to create stripes. Add 2 stripes on each side of box. Embroider mouth on any wide side of box, approx 4 sts above the base using Black, add French knots in Black on the White stripes for eyes.

Popcorn Topping

Row 1 (RS): Join Butter Brown to the first dc on top edge of box (as shown in chart) with 1BLss, [1ch, 1BLdc] in same st, 1BLdc in next 5 sts (6 sts).

Rows 2 to 6: 1ch (does not count as a st), turn, 1dc in every st (6 sts).

Embroider the square by covering it with French knots in Butter Brown to represent popcorn. Fasten off. Sew BLs of row 16 of box to row 1, using whipstitch. Sew base to sides. Stuff work, whipstitch BL of top edge to popcorn topping. Add extra French knots to cover any sewing if needed.

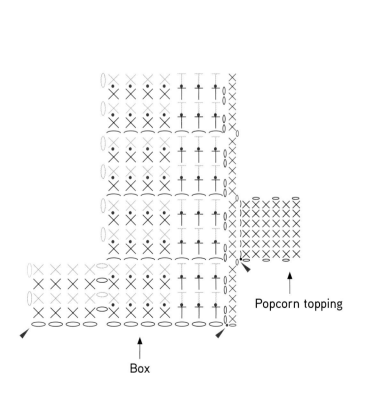

Popcorn topping

Box

BURGER

Materials

- 0.75mm-0.9mm (14/10 to 14/8 steel) crochet hook (0.9mm will produce slightly larger item)
- Gütermann top stitching thread in Butter Brown 893, Red 364, Light Green 152, Brown 650, Black 000
- Embroidery needle

Finished Size

14mm x 11mm x 11mm (³⁵⁄₆₄in x ⁷⁄₁₆in x ⁷⁄₁₆in)

Bread Bun (make 2)

Round 1: Using Butter Brown, make a magic ring, 6dc into ring, ss to first st to join (6 sts).

Round 2: 2dc in every st, ss to join (12 sts).

Round 3: [2dc in next st, 1dc] 6 times, ss to join (18 sts).

Round 4: 1dc in every st, ss to join.

Pause crocheting on 1 bread bun to embroider face, using Black make French knots on sts 4 and 9 of round 2 for eyes and embroider a mouth between the eyes.

Round 5: [1BLdc2tog, 1dc] 6 times (12 sts).

Round 6: [Dc2tog] 6 times (6 sts).

Minimal stuffing is required. Fasten off and sew in ends. Repeat in Brown for burger patty, no need to stuff.

Tomato

Using Red, repeat rounds 1 to 3 of bread bun.

Lettuce

Round 1: Using Light Green, make a magic ring, 6dc into ring, ss to join (6 sts).

Round 2: [1dc, 2ch, 1dc, 2ch] in every st (12 ch sps for lettuce frills).

Fasten off and sew in ends. Stack elements and sew into place.

CHICKEN DRUMSTICK

Materials

- 0.75mm-0.9mm (14/10 to 14/8 steel) crochet hook (0.9mm will produce slightly larger item)
- Gütermann top stitching thread in Butter Brown 893, White 111, Black 000
- Embroidery needle

Finished Size

20mm x 8mm x 8mm (²⁵⁄₃₂in x ⁵⁄₁₆in x ⁵⁄₁₆in)

Bone

Using White, make 6PCIC (see Crochet Techniques), [2ch, 1htr, ss, 2ch, 1htr, 2ch, ss] in sixth st to make bone shape, ss down side of 6 sts so that thread ends are positioned at the end of the bone. Fasten off.

Meat

Work in continuous rounds, starting with a magic ring in Butter Brown.

Round 1: 6dc into ring (6 sts).

Round 2: [2dc in next st, 1dc] 3 times (9 sts).

Round 3: [2dc in next st, 2dc] 3 times (12 sts).

Rounds 4 and 5: 1dc in every st.

Round 6: [Dc2tog, 2dc] 3 times (9 sts).

Round 7: [Dc2tog, 1dc] 3 times (6 sts).

Round 8: 1dc in every st.

Fasten off and stuff chicken leg, insert bone into the opening and sew into place using Butter Brown thread, securing the bone and closing opening at the same time. Embroider mouth and make French knots for eyes using Black thread.

COFFEE CUP

Materials

- 0.75mm-0.9mm (14/10 to 14/8 steel) crochet hook (0.9mm will produce slightly larger item)
- Gütermann top stitching thread in Blue 736, Light Brown 868, Black 000, Light Pink 758
- Embroidery needle

Finished Size

13mm x 13mm x 10mm ($^{33}\!/_{64}$in x $^{33}\!/_{64}$in x $^{25}\!/_{64}$in)

Coffee Top

Round 1: Using Light Brown, make a magic ring, 6dc into ring, ss to first st to join (6 sts).

Round 2: 1ch, [1dc, 2dc in next st] 3 times, ss to join (12 sts).

Fasten off and sew in ends.

Cup

Round 1: Using Blue, make a magic ring, 6dc into ring, ss to first st to join (6 sts).

Round 2: 2dc in every st, ss to join (12 sts).

Round 3: [2dc in next st, 1dc] 6 times, ss to join (18 sts).

Round 4: 1ch, 1BLdc in every st, ss to join.

Rounds 5 to 9: 1dc in every st, ss to join (18 sts).

Pause crocheting in Blue, whipstitch BL of round 9 to coffee top using Light Brown thread, joining 2 sts for every 1 st in coffee cup, stuff before closing fully.

Round 10: 1dc in every st, ss to join (18 sts).

To make handle, work 2ch, 1htr into same st, [2ch, 1htr in sp between htr and 2ch below] twice (makes a cord with 3 loops). Fasten off, sew end of handle to the cup body. Embroider mouth and eyes 3 sts apart using Black thread. Embroider cheeks using Light Pink.

PIZZA

Materials

- 0.75mm-0.9mm (14/10 to 14/8 steel) crochet hook (0.9mm will produce slightly larger item)
- Gütermann top stitching thread in Yellow 106, Light Brown 868, Black 000, Red 156
- Embroidery needle

Finished Size

20mm x 15mm x 3mm ($^{25}\!/_{32}$in x $^{19}\!/_{32}$in x $^{1}\!/_{8}$in)

Using Light Brown make 2ch.

Row 1 (RS): Starting in second ch from hook, 1dc (1 st).

Row 2: 1ch (does not count as a st throughout), turn, 2dc in next st (2 sts).

Row 3: 1ch, turn, 1dc in every st.

Row 4: 1ch, turn, 1dc, 2dc in next st (3 sts).

Row 5: 1ch, turn, 2dc, 2dc in next st (4 sts).

Row 6: 1ch, turn, 3dc, 2dc in next st (5 sts).

Row 7: 1ch, turn, 4dc, 2dc in next st (6 sts).

Rows 8 to 14: 1ch, turn, I dc in every st.

Fasten off but do not cut yarn. Change to Yellow, leaving a long end for crocheting edging later on.

Row 15: [1FLss, 1ch, 1FLdc] in first st, 1FLdc in every st (6 sts).

Row 16: 1ch, turn, 4dc, dc2tog (5 sts).

Row 17: 1ch, turn, 3dc, dc2tog (4 sts).

Row 18: 1ch, turn, 2dc, dc2tog (3 sts).

Row 19: 1ch, turn, 1dc, dc2tog (2 sts).

Row 20: 1ch, turn, 2dc.

Row 21: 1ch, turn, dc2tog, fasten off.

Pick up Yellow tail end from row 15, work 8dc up side of triangle, 3dc in tip, 8dc down side of triangle, change to Light Brown, work 13dc up side of Light Brown triangle, 3dc in triangle tip, 13dc down rem side.

Fasten off, sew in Light Brown thread ends on WS of rows 13 and 14 to add bulk to the crust and to save stuffing. Embroider face on lower end of Yellow triangle using Black. Embroider little circles in Red for pepperoni slices.

Fold in half, wrong sides together to make a triangle, line up 3dc from both tips of triangle. Use Yellow thread to whipstitch BLs together, use Light Brown thread to sew up openings on the crust.

Optional: sew a line of running stitches in Light Brown, where rows 14 and 15 meet, through both layers of crochet to add further definition to the crust.

CUPCAKE & ICE CREAM

Materials

- 0.75mm-0.9mm (14/10 to 14/8 steel) crochet hook (0.9mm will produce slightly larger item)
- Gütermann top stitching thread in Bright Pink 382 (for both)
- Gütermann top stitching thread in Light Pink 758, Ivory 414, Black 000 for Cupcake (C)
- Gütermann top stitching thread in Lilac 158, Light Brown 868, Black 000, White 111, Light Green 152, Blue 736, Yellow 106 for Ice Cream (IC)
- Embroidery needle

Finished Size

Cupcake 14mm x 10mm x 10mm (³⁵⁄₆₄in x ²⁵⁄₆₄in x ²⁵⁄₆₄in)

Ice Cream 21mm x 10mm x 10mm (⁵³⁄₆₄in x ²⁵⁄₆₄in x ²⁵⁄₆₄in)

Cherry

Using Bright Pink, make a magic ring, [3ch, 5BLtr] into ring to make bobble, fasten off, leaving a tail for sewing up.

Icing or Ice Cream Scoop

Work in continuous rounds, starting with a magic ring in Light Pink for cupcake (C) or Lilac for ice cream (IC).

Round 1: 6dc into ring (6 sts).

Round 2: 2dc in every st (12 sts).

Round 3: [2dc in next st, 3dc] 3 times (15 sts).

Round 4: 1dc in every st.

Round 5 (IC only): As round 4.

Pause crocheting to attach cherry. Thread end of the bobble through to the inside and knot it with the magic ring thread. Sew sides of bobble using Bright Pink to make it extra secure.

Round 5 (C) or 6 (IC): [Dc2tog, 3dc] 3 times (12 sts).

Round 6 (C) or 7 (IC): 1BLdc in every st.

Round 7 (C) or 8 (IC): [Dc2tog] 6 times (6 sts).

Stuff body, sew hole closed and fasten off.

Cupcake Casing

Round 1: Using Ivory, make a magic ring, 6dc into ring, ss to first st to join (6 sts).

Round 2: 1ch (does not count as a st throughout), 2dc in every st, ss to join (12 sts).

Round 3: 1ch, 1BLdc in every st, ss to join.

Round 4: 1ch, 1dc in every st.

Round 5: [ss, 1ch] in every st of round 4 together with the FLs of icing of round 6 (adds edging and joins case to icing sts).

Fasten off and sew in ends.

Ice Cream Cone

Work in continuous rounds, starting with a magic ring in Light Brown.

Round 1: 6dc into ring (6 sts).

Rounds 2 and 3: 1dc in every st.

Round 4: [2dc in next st, 1dc] 3 times (9 sts).

Round 5: 1dc in every st.

Round 6: [2dc in next st, 2dc] 3 times (12 sts).

Round 7: (Ss, 1ch) in every st of round 6 together with the FLs of ice cream scoop of round 7 (adds edging and joins cone to icing sts).

Fasten off and sew in ends.

Embroider eyes 3 sts apart with French knots in Black. Embroider little dashes in different colours for sprinkles (IC).

MILKSHAKE

Materials

- 0.75mm-0.9mm (14/10 to 14/8 steel) crochet hook (0.9mm will produce slightly larger item)
- Gütermann top stitching thread in Light Pink 758, White 111, Bright Pink 382, Black 000, Red 156
- Embroidery needle

Finished Size

24mm x 9mm x 9mm (15⁄16in x 23⁄64in x 23⁄64in)

Cherry

Work as cherry for cupcake and ice cream.

Straw

Work [2 forward knots in Red, 2 forward knots in White] twice, work 2 more forward knots in Red (see Crochet Techniques).

Cream Topping

Work in continuous rounds, starting with a magic ring in White.

Round 1: 6dc into ring (6 sts).

Round 2: 2dc in every st (12 sts).

Round 3: 1dc in every st, 1BLdc into next st to fasten off for a smoother finish.

Thread all 4 strands of straw through any round 1 st with a tilted position. Knot together with the magic ring thread of the cream topping to secure, thus saving sewing in lots of ends and the threads also act as stuffing.

Glass Base

Round 1: Using Light Pink make a magic ring, 8dc into ring, ss to join.

Round 2 (RS): [Ss, 1ch] in every st, ss to join.

Fasten off and sew in ends.

Glass Body

Work in continuous rounds, starting with a magic ring in Light Pink.

Round 1: 6dc into ring (6 sts).

Round 2: [2dc in next st, 1dc] 3 times (9 sts).

Round 3: [2dc in next st, 2dc] 3 times (12 sts).

Rounds 4 to 7: 1dc in every st.

Pause crocheting at round 7 to sew base to bottom of glass body, RS facing downwards. Stuff body.

Round 8: [Ss, 1ch] in every st of round 7 together with the FLs of cream topping in round 3. Add more stuffing as you go, especially to the underside of the cream topping. Fasten off and sew in ends.

Embroider French knots between rows 5 and 6 of glass body in Black for eyes, about 2 sts apart. Add a mouth using Black between eyes.

Animals

This chapter is certainly for pet lovers. Make your own tiny pets that you can carry around in your pocket, or hide them around the house to surprise your family or housemates. Try out different embroidery techniques for different levels of cuteness and expressiveness. You could even adapt the markings so that they resemble your pets at home.

Many of the patterns in this chapter crochet the limbs and the body together using bobble stitches, which in turn reduces the amount of sewing you need to do at the assembly stage, and who doesn't love that?

BUNNY

Materials

- 1.25mm-1.5mm (9/4 to 8/7/2 steel) crochet hook (1.5mm hook will produce slightly larger item)
- Scheepjes Sweet Treat in Colonial Rose (CR) 398, Bridal White 105, Jet Black 110, Ruby 517
- Embroidery needle

Finished Size

30mm x 18mm x 15mm (1³⁄₁₆in x ⁴⁵⁄₆₄in x ¹⁹⁄₃₂in)

Body and Head

Special stitches: bobble - 4 treble st bobble (see Crochet Techniques)

Work in continuous rounds, using Colonial Rose, make 6ch.

Round 1: Starting in second ch from hook, [1dc, 2dc in next st] twice, 4dc in last ch, working on other side of foundation ch, [2dc in next st, 1dc] twice, 2dc in beg ch (18 sts).

Round 2: 1bobble, 5dc, 1bobble, 5dc, 1bobble in Bridal White (tail), 5dc in CR (16 dc, 2 bobbles for feet, 1 bobble for tail). Fasten off Bridal White.

Rounds 3 and 4: 1dc in every st.

Round 5: 1dc, 1bobble, 5dc, 1bobble, 10dc (16 dc, 2 bobbles for arms).

Rounds 6 to 9: 1dc in every st (18 sts).

Round 10: [Dc2tog, 1dc] 6 times (12 sts). Stuff work.

Round 11: [Dc2tog] 6 times (6 sts). Sew hole closed and fasten off.

Ear (make 2)

Using CR make 4PCIC (see Crochet Techniques), or [4ch, 1 turning ch], crochet the following in single loops along the PCIC: ss, ss, 1dc, 3htr, continue along other side of PCIC: 1dc, ss, ss, ss in beg ch.

Fasten off, use thread tails to sew onto side of head at round 10.

Muzzle

Using Bridal White, make a magic ring, into the ring work 1ch, 2htr, 1ch, ss, ss, 1ch, 2htr, 1ch, ss, to make a small bow shape. Fasten off.

Using Ruby, sew through the magic ring and over the last ss to make the nose. Sew muzzle onto body between arms, on rounds 6 and 7. Add French knots in Jet Black or beads to either side for eyes.

DOG

Materials

- 1.25mm-1.5mm (9/4 to 8/7/2 steel) crochet hook (1.5mm hook will produce slightly larger item)
- Scheepjes Sweet Treat in Bluebird (B) 247, Bridal White (W) 105, Jet Black 110, Watermelon 252
- Embroidery needle

Finished Size

25mm x 18mm x 15mm (⁶³⁄₆₄in x ⁴⁵⁄₆₄in x ¹⁹⁄₃₂in)

Body and Head

Using B throughout, work as for bunny body and head rounds 1 to 6.

Rounds 7 and 8: 6dc in B, 7dc in W, 5dc in B.

Round 9: 6dc in B, 6dc in W, 6dc in B.

Round 10: [Dc2tog, 1dc] in B twice, [dc2tog, 1dc] in W twice, [dc2tog, 1dc] in B twice (12 sts). Stuff work.

Round 11: [Dc2tog] in B twice, [dc2tog] in W twice, [dc2tog] in B twice (6 sts). Fasten off and sew in ends.

Ears (make 1 in B and 1 in W)

Work as for bunny ears, but sew to side of head facing downwards.

Muzzle

Work as for bunny muzzle in B.

Sew a nose in Jet Black and add French knots or beads in Jet Black for the eyes. Embroider a tongue and cheeks in Watermelon.

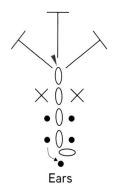

Ears

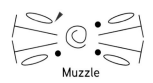

Muzzle

PIG

Materials

- 1.25mm-1.5mm (9/4 to 8/7/2 steel) crochet hook (1.5mm hook will produce slightly larger item)
- Scheepjes Sweet Treat in Watermelon 252, Jet Black 110, Colonial Rose 398
- Embroidery needle

Finished Size

25mm x 18mm x 15mm ($^{63}/_{64}$in x $^{45}/_{64}$in x $^{19}/_{32}$in)

Body and Head

Work as for bunny body and head to round 9 (18 sts).

Round 10: [1BLdc, (dc2tog, 1dc) twice, dc2tog] twice (12 sts).

Round 11: [Dc2tog] 6 times (6 sts).

Fasten off and sew in ends.

Ears (make 2)

Working into one of the FLs from round 10 in Watermelon: [ss, 2ch, 1htr, 2ch, 1htr, 2ch, ss] all in same FL. Fasten off and weave in ends. Repeat for other ear in other FL.

Tail

Work 11PCIC (see Crochet Techniques), fasten off. Twist into 2 loops and sew onto back of pig on round 2.

Nose

Using Watermelon, embroider a rectangle shape with long stitches between the arms on rounds 4 to 6. Whipstitch around the 2 side sts of the rectangle. This makes an even rectangle shape with the illusion of satin sts. Using Jet Black add 2 sts for the nostrils, and French knots on either side for the eyes. Embroider cheeks under the eyes in Colonial Rose.

COW

Materials

- 1.25mm-1.5mm (9/4 to 8/7/2 steel) crochet hook (1.5mm hook will produce slightly larger item)
- Scheepjes Sweet Treat in Bridal White 105, Amethyst 240, Jet Black 110, Watermelon 252
- Embroidery needle

Finished Size

25mm x 18mm x 15mm ($^{63}/_{64}$in x $^{45}/_{64}$in x $^{19}/_{32}$in)

Body and Head

Work as for pig body and head in Bridal White, with ears and nose in Amethyst. Embroider spots all over the body in Amethyst.

Horns (make 2)

Using Watermelon, work 2PCIC (see Crochet Techniques), or 3ch, 1dc in 2nd and 3rd ch away from hook. Fasten off and sew onto head at round 10, with the same spacing as the eyes.

ROBIN

Materials

- 1.25mm-1.5mm (9/4 to 8/7/2 steel) crochet hook (1.5mm hook will produce slightly larger item)
- Scheepjes Sweet Treat in Bridal White 105, Topaz (T) 179, Hot Red (R) 115, Moon Rock 254, Jet Black 110
- Embroidery needle

Finished Size

18mm x 20mm x 20mm (⁴⁵⁄₆₄in x ²⁵⁄₃₂in x ²⁵⁄₃₂in)

Body

Work in continuous rounds, starting with a magic ring in Bridal White.

Round 1: 6dc into ring (6 sts).

Round 2: 2dc in every st (12 sts).

Round 3: 3ch (does not count as a st), [1tr, 1htr, 1dc] in first st, [1dc, 2dc in next st] 5 times, [1dc, 1htr, 1tr] in last st, ss to top of beg 3ch (21 sts).

Change to Topaz.

Round 4: Starting in last st of round 3, loosely work 1BLss in every st (21 sts).

Round 5: Work this round into round 4 ss and round 3 BLs joining them together, 7dc in T, 7dc in R, 7dc in T.

Round 6: Dc2tog in T, 5dc in T, 7dc in R, 5dc in T, dc2tog in T (19 sts).

Round 7: Dc2tog in T, 4dc in T, 7dc in R, 4dc in T, dc2tog in T (17 sts).

Round 8: Dc2tog in T, 3dc in T, [1dc in R, dc2tog in R] twice, 1dc in R, 3dc in T, dc2tog in T (13 sts).

Stuff work.

Round 9: 4dc in T, 5dc in R, 4dc in T.

Fasten off R, continue with T only.

Round 10: 4dc, 5BLdc, 4dc.

Round 11: 1dc, [dc2tog] 6 times (7 sts).

Fasten off and sew in ends.

Wing (make 2)

Using Topaz, make a magic ring, work [1ch, 2dc, 1htr, 1tr, 1ttr, 1tr, 1htr, 2dc] into ring, pull closed and ss to first dc.

Sew wings to sides of body. Using Moon Rock, sew 2 long sts next to the wings at the bottom of the Hot Red patch. Use same thread to sew a triangle for the beak, at rounds 8 to 9. Whipstitch the long threads together to fill in the triangle and give a 3D effect. Embroider French knots for the eyes using Jet Black.

HAMSTER

Materials

- 1.25mm-1.5mm (9/4 to 8/7/2 steel) crochet hook (1.5mm hook will produce slightly larger item)
- Scheepjes Sweet Treat in Bridal White (W) 105, Topaz (T) 179, Jet Black 110, Watermelon 252, Colonial Rose 398
- Embroidery needle

Finished Size

25mm x 15mm x 15mm (⁶³⁄₆₄in x ¹⁹⁄₃₂in x ¹⁹⁄₃₂in)

Body and Head

Work in continuous rounds, using Topaz make 6ch.

Special stitches: bobble – 4 treble st bobble (see Crochet Techniques)

Round 1: Starting in second ch from hook, [1dc, 2dc in next st] twice, 4dc in last ch, working on other side of foundation ch, [2dc in next st, 1dc] twice, 2dc in beg ch (18 sts).

Round 2: 1bobble in T, 1dc in T, 3dc in W, 1dc in T, 1bobble in T, 5dc in T, 1bobble in T, 5dc in T (15 dc, 2 bobble feet, 1 bobble tail).

Round 3: 2dc in T, 3dc in W, 13dc in T (18 sts).

Round 4: 1dc in T, 5dc in W, 12dc in T.

Round 5: 1dc in T, 1bobble in T, 4dc in W, 1bobble in T, 11dc in T (16 dc, 2 bobble arms).

Round 6: 1dc in T, 6dc in W, 11dc in T.

Fasten off W, continue with T only.

Round 7: 1dc in every st.

Round 8: [8dc, (ss, 1ch, 1dc, 1ch, ss) in next st] twice (16 dc, 2 ears)

Stuff work.

Round 9: [(Dc2tog, 1dc) twice, dc2tog, skip ear] twice (10 sts).

Round 10: [Dc2tog] 5 times (5 sts).

Sew opening closed and fasten off. Embroider nose just above Bridal White sts on round 6 using Watermelon, sew eyes using Jet Black on either side of round 7, just above the nose. Add cheeks in Colonial Rose.

GREEN PARROT

Materials

- 1.25mm-1.5mm (9/4 to 8/7/2 steel) crochet hook (1.5mm hook will produce slightly larger item)
- Scheepjes Sweet Treat in Sage Green 212, Watermelon 252, Topaz 179, Hot Red 115
- Embroidery needle
- 2mm black eye beads and cotton thread for sewing

Finished Size

25mm x 18mm x 27mm (6¾⁄₆₄in x 4⅝⁄₆₄in x 1¹⁄₁₆in)

Body

Work in continuous rounds, starting with a magic ring in Sage Green.

Round 1: 6dc into ring (6 sts).

Round 2: 2dc in every st (12 sts).

Round 3: [3dc, 2BLdc in next st] 3 times (15 sts).

Rounds 4 to 7: 1dc in every st.

Round 8: [3dc, dc2tog] 3 times (12 sts).

Rounds 9 and 10: 1dc in every st.

Stuff work.

Round 11: [Dc2tog] 6 times (6 sts).

Fasten off and sew hole closed.

Tail

Work in continuous rounds, starting with a magic ring in Sage Green.

Round 1: 6dc into ring (6 sts).

Round 2: [2dc in next st, 2dc] twice (8 sts).

Round 3: 1dc in every st.

Round 4: [Dc2tog, 2dc] twice (6 sts).

Round 5: 1dc in every st.

Flatten opening and sew closed. Attach to 1 pair of the FLs on body in round 3.

Wing (make 2)

Using Sage Green, make a magic ring, work [1ch, 2dc, 1htr, 1tr, 1dtr, 1ttr, 1dtr, 1tr, 1htr, 2dc] into ring, pull closed, ss to first dc. Fasten off and sew to sides of body.

Feet (make 2)

Special stitches: bobble – 4 treble st bobble (see Crochet Techniques)

Working into one of the pairs of FLs on body in round 3 in Watermelon: [ss, 3ch, 1bobble] in FL, fasten off. Use tail end on top of bobble to sew to base of st to fold and flatten out the foot shape. Sew in ends. Repeat for other foot in the other pair of FLs.

Using Watermelon, sew a running st along round 7 to separate the head and body. Whipstitch around the running stitch to make the line more defined and cover any gaps in the stitching.

Beak

Sew a triangle shape that overlaps the neck line using Topaz. Whipstitch around sides of the triangle to fill it in and add a 3D effect. Add a couple of stitches above the triangle in Hot Red.

Attach eye beads on either side of the triangle for the eyes.

Wing

CHICKEN

Materials

- 1.25mm-1.5mm (9/4 to 8/7/2 steel) crochet hook (1.5mm hook will produce slightly larger item)
- Scheepjes Sweet Treat in Rust 388, Bridal White 105, Hot Red 115, Yellow Gold 208
- Embroidery needle
- 2mm black eye beads and cotton thread for sewing

Finished Size

20mm x 18mm x 20mm (²⁵⁄₃₂in x ⁴⁵⁄₆₄in x ²⁵⁄₃₂in)

Body

Work in continuous rounds, starting with a magic ring in Rust.

Round 1: 6dc into ring (6 sts).

Round 2: 2dc in every st (12 sts).

Round 3: [2dc in next st, 1dc] 6 times (18 sts).

Round 4: [1BLdc, 1dc] 9 times.

Rounds 5 and 6: 1dc in every st.

Fasten off and flatten work, line up the 18th st with the first st and 17th st with second st, sew them together. This makes the tail end and leaves 14 sts for crocheting the head.

Change to Bridal White.

Round 7: Starting at the tail end, 1BLss in every st (14 sts).

Round 8: Work 1dc in BL of each ss of round 7 and each BL of round 6 joining them together (14 sts).

Round 8: 1dc in every st.

Round 9: [Dc2tog] 7 times (7 sts).

Fasten off and sew in ends.

Crown

Using Hot Red, make a magic ring, into the ring work [1ch, 3dc, 1ch, ss], fasten off and use tail ends to sew onto chicken head.

Beak

Using Yellow Gold, ss into one White FL at front of head, 2ch, fasten off. Sew ends back into chicken head.

Left Wing

Using Rust, join to third Rust FL to left of beak, working with tail facing downwards, [ss, 1dc, 1htr, 1tr] in same st, [1dtr, 1tr, 2ch, ss] in next st, fasten off and sew in ends.

Right Wing

Using Rust, join to fourth Rust FL to right of beak, working with beak facing downward, [ss, 2ch, 1tr, 1dtr] in same st, [1tr, 1htr, 1dc, ss] in next st, fasten off and sew in ends.

Embroider chin in Hot Red and sew beads onto head for eyes.

CAT

Materials

- 1.25mm-1.5mm (9/4 to 8/7/2 steel) crochet hook (1.5mm hook will produce slightly larger item)
- Scheepjes Sweet Treat in Candle Light (C) 101, Topaz (T) 179, Jet Black 110, Colonial Rose 398
- Embroidery needle

Finished Size

23mm x 15mm x 15mm (²⁹⁄₃₂in x ¹⁹⁄₃₂in x ¹⁹⁄₃₂in)

Body and Head

Work in continuous rounds, using Topaz make 6ch.

Special stitches: bobble – 4 treble st bobble (see Crochet Techniques)

Round 1: Starting in second ch from hook, [1dc, 2dc in next st] twice, 4dc in last ch, working on other side of foundation ch, [2dc in next st, 1dc] twice, 2dc in beg ch (18 sts).

Round 2: 1bobble in T, 1dc in T, 3dc in C, 1dc in T, 1bobble in T, 11dc in T (16 dc, 2 bobble feet).

Round 3: 2dc in T, 4dc in C, 6dc in T, 4dc in C, 2dc in T (18 sts).

Round 4: 3dc in T, 3dc in C, 5dc in T, 6dc in C, 1dc in T.

Round 5: 2dc in T, 1bobble in T, 3dc in C, 1bobble in T, 11dc in T (16 sts, 2 bobble arms).

Round 6: 10dc in C, 6dc in T, 2dc in C.

Round 7: 2dc in T, 4dc in C, 12dc in T.

Round 8: 2dc in T, dc2tog in T, 1dc in C, dc2tog in C, [3dc in T, dc2tog in T] twice, 1dc (14 sts).

Ears

Work in rows to join top of head together and make ears.

Row 9: 1dc, flatten opening and line up sts so that the 1dc just worked is on the end, [1dc, 2ch, 1dc] in next st together with st behind it to make first ear, ss in FL of front row and BL of back row together across next 4 sts, [1dc, 2ch, 1dc] in next st together with st behind it to make second ear. Fasten off, sew end through rem dc to finish.

Embroider eyes between rounds 6 and 7 in Jet Black and add a nose between them in Colonial Rose.

SQUIRREL

Materials

- 1.25mm-1.5mm (9/4 to 8/7/2 steel) crochet hook (1.5mm hook will produce slightly larger item)
- Scheepjes Sweet Treat in Rust (R) 388, Topaz (T) 179, Colonial Rose 398
- Embroidery needle
- 2mm black eye beads and cotton thread for sewing

Finished Size

25mm x 18mm x 15mm (6³⁄₆₄in x 4⁵⁄₆₄in x 1⁹⁄₃₂in)

Body and Head

Special stitches: bobble – 4 treble st bobble (see Crochet Techniques)

Work in continuous rounds, using Rust make 6ch.

Round 1: Starting in second ch from hook, [1dc, 2dc in next st] twice, 4dc in last ch, working on other side of foundation ch, [2dc in next st, 1dc] twice, 2dc in beg ch (18 sts).

Round 2: 1bobble in R, 1dc in R, 3dc in T, 1dc in R, 1bobble in R, 11dc in R (16dc, 2 bobble feet).

Round 3: 2dc in R, 4dc in T, 12dc in R (18 sts).

Round 4: 2dc in R, 5dc in T, 11dc in R.

Round 5: 1dc in R, 1bobble in R, 1dc in R, 3dc in T, 1dc in R, 1bobble in R, 10dc in R (16dc, 2 bobble arms).

Fasten off T, continue with R only.

Rounds 6 and 7: 1dc in every st (18 sts).

Stuff work.

Round 8: 1dc, dc2tog, 3dc, dc2tog, 2dc, dc2tog, 3dc, dc2tog, 1dc (14 sts).

Ears

Work in rows to join top of head together and make ears.

Row 9: 1dc, flatten opening and line up sts so that the 1dc just worked is on the end, [1dc, 2ch, 1dc] in next st together with st behind it to make first ear, ss in FL of front row and BL of back row together across next 4 sts, [1dc, 2ch, 1dc] in next st together with st behind it to make second ear. Fasten off, sew end through rem dc to finish.

Tail

Work in continuous rounds, starting with a magic ring in Rust.

Round 1: 6dc into ring (6 sts).

Round 2: [1dc, 2dc in next st] 3 times (9 sts).

Round 3: [2dc, 2dc in next st] 3 times (12 sts).

Round 4: [3dc, 2dc in next st] 3 times (15 sts).

Rounds 5 to 7: 1dc in every st.

Round 8: [Dc2tog, 3dc] 3 times (12 sts).

Rounds 9 to 11: 1dc in every st.

Round 12: [Dc2tog, 4dc] twice (10 sts).

Round 13: 1dc in every st.

Fasten off, flatten opening and sew closed, fold the other end in half at the widest point to make the curl in the tail. Sew into place. Sew tail to the back of the squirrel.

Embroider a nose in the centre of round 6 using Colonial Rose and add beads on either side for the eyes.

Back to School

This chapter is for those who loved getting their new stationery together and breaking out the glitter gel pens for going back to school. It features an amigurumi book cover, which you can fill with your own paper pages, and little bags for any stowaway amigurumi! You can increase the thread and hook size to make different sized books and bags, to fit in even more amigurumi.

The projects in this chapter would make lovely gifts for teachers, school-starters and university-goers alike. They are crocheted using a 0.75mm (14/10 steel) hook and Gütermann top stitching thread but will work well with any type of crochet thread.

APPLE

Materials

- 0.75mm-0.9mm (14/10 to 14/8 steel) crochet hook (0.9mm will produce slightly larger item)
- Gütermann top stitching thread in Bright Red 156, Emerald Green 237, Dark Red 368, Black 000
- Embroidery needle

Finished Size

12mm x 8mm x 8mm ($^{15}\!/_{32}$in x $^{5}\!/_{16}$in x $^{5}\!/_{16}$in)

Stalk

Using Dark Red, make 4PCIC (see Crochet Techniques) or [4ch, 1 turning ch], turn, 4dc, fasten off.

Leaf

Using Emerald Green, make a magic ring, into ring work [1ch, 1htr, 2ch, ss in htr, 1ch, ss], fasten off.

Apple

Work in continuous rounds, starting with a magic ring in Bright Red.

Round 1: 6dc into ring (6 sts).

Round 2: 2dc in every st (12 sts).

Round 3: [2dc in next st, 2dc] 4 times (16 sts).

Pause crocheting in Bright Red, thread the ends from the leaf and stem through the magic ring of round 1 and secure from the inside of the apple.

Rounds 4 to 6: 1dc in every st.

Round 7: [Dc2tog, 2dc] 4 times (12 sts).

Stuff work

Round 8: [Dc2tog] 6 timed (6 sts).

Fasten off and sew opening closed, use rem thread to sew through to the top of the apple and back down again, pulling it taut to give a squished dimpled shape.

Using Black, embroider a face onto the apple, using French knots for eyes.

PEN

Materials

- 0.75mm-0.9mm (14/10 to 14/8 steel) crochet hook (0.9mm will produce slightly larger item)
- Gütermann top stitching thread in Lilac 158, Purple 810, Black 000; DMC Light Effects in Gold E3821
- Embroidery needle

Finished Size

27mm x 8mm x 6mm (1$^{1}\!/_{16}$in x $^{5}\!/_{16}$in x $^{15}\!/_{64}$in)

Pen

Work in continuous rounds, starting with a magic ring in Lilac.

Round 1: 6dc into ring (6 sts).

Round 2: 2dc in every st (12 sts).

Rounds 3 to 8: 1dc in every st.

Change to Purple, do not fasten off Lilac.

Round 9: 1dc in every st.

Change back to Lilac.

Round 10: 1BLdc in every st.

Rounds 11 to 13: 1dc in every st.

Ss in next st before fastening off Lilac, change to Purple.

Round 14: [1BLdc, BLdc2tog] 4 times (8 sts).

Round 15: [2dc, dc2tog] twice (6 sts).

Round 16: [Dc2tog] 3 times (3 sts).

Fasten off and sew in ends.

Pen Clip

Using Purple, make 7PCIC (see Crochet Techniques), fasten off and use ends to sew onto side of pen, covering the colour changes in the previous rounds. Embroider face using Black with French knots 3 sts apart on round 9. Using Gold (stranded into one singular starnd) embroider a line of running sts between rounds 13 and 14.

CALCULATOR

Materials

- 0.75mm-0.9mm (14/10 to 14/8 steel) crochet hook (0.9mm will produce slightly larger item)
- Gütermann top stitching thread in Caribbean Blue (B) 736, White (W) 111, Black 000, Dark Blue 232, Mid Grey 701
- Embroidery needle

Finished Size

15mm x 10mm x 6mm (¹⁹⁄₃₂in x ²⁵⁄₆₄in x ¹⁵⁄₆₄in)

Using Caribbean Blue, make 6ch or 5PCIC (see Crochet Techniques), 1ch.

Round 1: Starting in second ch from hook, 2dc in ch, 1dc in next 3 ch, 4dc in last ch, working on other side of ch, 1dc in next 3 ch, 2dc in last ch (14 sts).

Rounds 2 to 6: Working in continuous rounds, 1dc in every st.

Rounds 7 and 8: 2dc in B, 5dc in W, 7dc in B.

Fasten off W, continue in B only.

Round 9: 3dc in B, 4BLdc in B to make straighter edge at top of calculator.

Fasten off. Embroider eyes using French knots and a mouth on the screen in Black. Add little buttons using Dark Blue and Mid Grey thread. Stuffing may not be needed depending on the bulk created from the embroidery. Sew top opening closed.

LAPTOP

Materials

- 0.75mm-0.9mm (14/10 to 14/8 steel) crochet hook (0.9mm will produce slightly larger item)
- Gütermann top stitching thread in Mid Grey 701, Light Grey 008, Black 000, Pale Pink 758
- Embroidery needle
- Cardboard for stiffening sides of laptop (optional)

Finished Size

25mm x 18mm x 3mm (⁶³⁄₆₄in x ⁴⁵⁄₆₄in x ⅛in)

Using Mid Grey, make 11ch.

Row 1: Starting in second ch from hook, 10dc (10 sts).

Rows 2 to 7: 1ch (does not count as a stitch throughout), turn, 10dc (10 sts).

Row 8: 1ch, turn, 10BLdc.

Rows 9 to 14: 1ch, turn, 10dc.

Row 15: 1ch, turn, 10FLdc.

Row 16: 1ch, turn, 10BLdc.

Rows 17 to 22: 1ch, turn, 10dc.

Row 23: 1ch, turn, 10FLdc.

Rows 24 to 28: 1ch, turn, 1dc, change to Light Grey, 8dc, change back to Mid Grey, 1dc (10 sts).

Row 29: 1ch, turn, 10dc in Mid Grey.

Fasten off and leave long threads for sewing.

This makes one long strip with 4 panels and one narrow panel in the middle for the spine. Embroider detailing such as keys in Black and heart in Pale Pink on the laptop keyboard and screen. Add French knots for the eyes in Black, embroider a Black mouth and Pale Pink cheeks on the outside of the laptop.

Sides can be reinforced with small rectangles of card (or plastic) to keep the panels flat. Fold panels inwards to make the laptop shape. Stitch the sides together to finish.

SATCHEL

Materials

- 0.75mm-0.9mm (14/10 to 14/8 steel) crochet hook (0.9mm will produce slightly larger item)
- Gütermann top stitching thread in Chocolate Brown 650, Black 000, Light Pink 758
- Embroidery needle
- 2 x 3mm round beads

Finished Size

20mm x 24mm x 7mm (²⁵⁄₃₂in x ¹⁵⁄₁₆in x ⁹⁄₃₂in)

Satchel

This is a functional mini bag that can carry your other crocheted items in! it is designed to house the laptop.

Using Chocolate Brown, make 11ch.

Round 1: Starting in second ch from hook, 2dc in ch, 1dc next 8 ch, 4dc in last ch, working on other side of foundation ch, 1dc in next 8 ch, 2dc in last ch, ss to join (24 sts).

Round 2: 1ch (does not count as a st throughout), 2dc next 2 sts, 8dc, 2dc in next 4 sts, 8dc, 2dc next 2 sts, ss to join (32 sts).

Work in continuous rounds from this point on, marking the end of each round as you go.

Round 3: 1ch, 1BLdc in every st (32 sts).

Rounds 4 to 10: 1dc in every st.

Flap

Work in rows, turning at the end of each row.

Rows 11 to 18: 1ch, turn, 1dc next 13 sts.

Flap Fastenings

Starting on row 14 of the flap, in second st from the edge using Chocolate Brown, work surface ss to flap edge, make 7ch, work ss from flap edge back to row 14. Check that the loop is the right size for your chosen bead fastenings before fastening off and sewing in ends. Add or reduce the number of ch if needed. Repeat for other side of flap.

Strap

Using Chocolate Brown join with a ss to row 10, 2 sts away from the edge of the flap, 2ch, 1tr in same st (makes loop), [2ch, 1tr in loop] 25 times or more if you require a longer strap. Fasten off and sew end of strap onto the opposite side of round 10, 2 sts away from the bag flap.

Embroider face on the bag flap using Black and Light Pink and sew beads onto the front of the bag to line up with the fastenings.

EXERCISE BOOK

Materials

- 0.75mm-0.9mm (14/10 to 14/8 steel) crochet hook (0.9mm will produce slightly larger item)
- Gütermann top stitching thread in Blue 322; Gütermann hand quilting cotton in White 5709 (or small rectangular pieces of white felt for book pages)
- Embroidery needle
- 1 x 2mm round bead

Finished Size

15mm x 14mm x 7mm (¹⁹⁄₃₂in x ³⁵⁄₆₄in x ⁹⁄₃₂in)

Book

Using Blue, make 10ch.

Row 1: Starting in second ch from hook, 9dc (9 sts).

Rows 2 to 7: 1ch (does not count as a st throughout), turn, 9dc in every st.

Row 8: 1ch, turn, 9BLdc.

Row 9: 1ch, turn, 9dc.

Row 10: As row 8.

Rows 11 to 15: As row 2.

Row 16: 1ch, turn, 5dc, 10ch, ss into 7th ch from hook and rem 3 ch, 1dc in each rem st of row 15 (9 sts, 1 fastening).

Check that the hole for the fastening is a suitable size for your chosen bead and adjust the number of ch accordingly. Fasten off and sew in ends.

Page (make 2)

Alternative: cut out 2 pieces of white felt instead of crocheting pages.

Using White, make 17ch.

Row 1: starting in second ch from hook, 1dc next 8 ch, 1ch, 1dc in rem 8 ch (16 sts)

Rows 2 to 11: 1ch (does not count as a st throughout), turn, 8dc, 1ch, 8dc.

Fasten off. Fold pages in half, place side by side and sew into the spine of the book cover. Sew a bead onto the front cover and embroider a little oval for the label in White.

TEXTBOOK

Materials

- 0.75mm-0.9mm (14/10 to 14/8 steel) crochet hook (0.9mm will produce slightly larger item)
- Gütermann top stitching thread in Emerald 237, Butter Brown 893, Black 000, Light Pink 758
- Embroidery needle
- White paper

Finished Size

20mm x 16mm x 17mm (²⁵⁄₃₂in x ⁵⁄₈in x ⁴³⁄₆₄in)

Book

Using Emerald, make 37ch.

Row 1: Starting in second ch from hook, 1dc in first 7 ch, 1ch, 1dc in next 9 ch, 1ch, 1dc in next 4 ch (makes spine), 1ch, 1dc in next 9 ch, 1ch, 1dc in rem 7 ch (36 sts, 4 ch sp).

Rows 2 to 8: 1ch (does not count as a st), turn, 7dc, 1ch, 9dc, 1ch, 4dc, 1ch, 9dc, 1ch, 7dc.

Change to Butter Brown on last st of row 8.

Rows 9 to 11: As row 2 using Butter Brown (36 sts).

Change to Emerald.

Rows 12 and 13: As row 2 using Emerald.

This makes a long rectangle with 2 main panels, 1 narrow panel (book spine), plus 2 more fold under panels.

Embroider =%+ or any other desired symbols onto the Butter Brown stripe using Black. Embroider a face below it using Black for the eyes and mouth and Light Pink for the cheeks, placing the eyes on sts 3 and 7 of row 5.

Fold the outer 2 panels into the centre 2 panels to make the book sleeve shape. Sew the side edges closed, leaving an opening for inserting the pages.

Pages

Cut long strips of paper 2cm (¾in) thick, score in 12mm (½in) intervals. Fold into a concertina pattern. Glue extra strips onto the end and continue the process until it matches the thickness of the spine. To finish, insert the first and the last pages into the sleeves of the book.

BACKPACK

Materials

- 0.75mm-0.9mm (14/10 to 14/8 steel) crochet hook (0.9mm will produce slightly larger item)
- Gütermann top stitching thread in Dark Blue 232, Mid Blue 322, Mustard 412, Butter Brown 893
- Embroidery needle
- 1 x 4mm round bead

Finished Size

30mm x 25mm x 15mm (1³⁄₁₆in x ⁶³⁄₆₄in x ¹⁹⁄₃₂in)

Strap (make 2)

Row 1: Using Dark Blue make 4ch, 1tr in first st (makes loop), [3ch, 1tr in loop] 8 times (9 loops).

Round 2: Working along edge of row 1, 1ch (does not count as a st), 3dc in each of next 8 loops, [3dc, 2ch, 1dc, 2ch, 3ch] in ninth loop, 3dc along other side in each of 7 loops, [3dc, 2ch, 1dc] in last loop, ss to first dc to join (56 dc).

Fasten off and sew in ends.

Bag Base

Using Dark Blue make 7ch.

Round 1: Starting in second ch from hook, 2dc in ch, 1dc in next 4 ch, 4dc in last ch, working on other side of foundation ch, 1dc in next 4 ch, 2dc in last ch, ss to join (16 sts).

Round 2: 1ch (does not count as a st throughout), 2dc in first 2 sts, 4dc, 2dc in next 4 sts, 4dc, 2dc in next 2 sts, ss to first st (24 sts).

Round 3: 1ch, 2dc in next 4 sts, 4dc, 2dc in next 8 sts, 4dc, 2dc in last 4 sts, ss to first st (40 sts).

Round 4: 1ch, 1BLdc in every st, ss to join.

Rounds 5 to 7: 1ch, 1dc in every st, ss to join.

Change to Mid Blue, starting next round on fifth st of prev round. This positions any visible joins to back of bag and will be hidden by sewing on the strap.

Rounds 8 to 10: Ss, 1ch, [2dc in Mid Blue, 2dc in Mustard] 10 times.

Change back to Dark Blue.

Round 11: 1BLss in first st of prev round, 1BLdc in every st, ss to join (40 sts).

Change to Butter Brown, work in continuous rounds from this point onwards.

Rounds 12 to 23: 1dc in every st.

Round 24: [2dc, 2ch, skip 2 sts] 10 times (20 sts, 20 ch sps).

Round 25: [2dc, 2dc in ch sp] 10 times (40 sts). Fasten off.

Bag Flap

Row 1: Using Mid Blue, [1BLss, 1ch, 1dc] in third st of prev round, 1dc in next 11 sts (12 sts).

Rows 2 to 8: 1ch (does not count as a st throughout), turn, 12dc.

Row 9: 1ch, turn, dc2tog, 8dc, dc2tog (10 sts).

Row 10: 1ch, turn, dc2tog, 3dc, 8ch, 3dc, dc2tog (8 sts, 1 button loop).

Check that the button loop is the right size for your chosen bead, adapt the number of ch accordingly.

Fasten off.

Drawstring

Using Dark Blue, make 90ch (check length and adapt number of ch to desired length), fasten off and knot both ends. Starting at the front of the bag, weave the drawstring through the holes made in round 24, leaving long ends at the front.

Sew bead to the front of the bag. Position at the centre of the first Butter Brown row. Sew the bottom of the straps to the base of the bag into the FLs on round 4, and the tops of the straps to the FLs at the top of the flap. The outer edge of the straps should line up with the outer edge of the bag flap.

LUNCH BOX

Materials

- 0.75mm-0.9mm (14/10 to 14/8 steel) crochet hook (0.9mm will produce slightly larger item)
- Gütermann top stitching thread in Lilac 158, Bright Pink 382, Green 235, Black 000
- Embroidery needle

Finished Size

17mm x 17mm x 12mm (⁴³⁄₆₄in x ⁴³⁄₆₄in x ¹⁵⁄₃₂in)

Side (make 2)

The lunch box is made by making each half and then sewing them together.

Using Lilac make 8ch.

Rows 1 to 8: 1ch (does not count as a st throughout), turn, 1dc in every st (7 sts).

Round 1: Do not turn work, 1dc in each row edge down side of work (8 dc), 2dc in first st of bottom edge for corner, 1dc in next 5 sts, 2dc in last st for corner, 1dc in next 8 rows up side of work, 2dc in first st along top for corner, 1dc in next 5 sts, 2dc in last st for corner (34 sts).

Round 2: 1BLdc in every st.

Round 3: 1dc in every st.

Round 4: Using Bright Pink surface crochet in every st of round 2, just behind the FLs.

Embroider a face on one side with rows 1 to 8 of the face positioned vertically. Embroider French knots using Black to make the eyes, 4 rows apart. Add Bright Pink cheeks using the end threads from round 4 and add a little Black 'V' shape in the middle to make the smile.

Using Green, whipstitch the FLs of round 3 to join the 2 sides together, stuffing as you go, work 7PCIC (see Crochet Techniques) in Green to make the lunch box handle and sew on the top.

PENCIL

Materials

- 0.75mm-0.9mm (14/10 to 14/8 steel) crochet hook (0.9mm will produce slightly larger item)
- Gütermann top stitching thread in Light Pink 758, Mid Grey 701, Butter Brown 893, Yellow 106, Black 000
- Embroidery needle

Finished Size

30mm x 6mm x 6mm (1³⁄₁₆in x ¹⁵⁄₆₄in x ¹⁵⁄₆₄in)

Work in continuous rounds, starting with a magic ring in Butter Brown.

Round 1: 6dc into ring (6 sts).

Round 2: 1dc in every st.

Round 3: [2dc in next st, 2dc] twice (8 sts).

Round 4: 1dc in every st.

Round 5: [2dc in next st, 1dc] 4 times (12 sts).

Ss in next st, then change to Yellow.

Round 6: 1BLdc in every st.

Rounds 7 to 14: 1dc in every st.

Ss in next st, then change to Mid Grey.

Round 15: 1dc in every st, ss to first st to join

Change to Light Pink.

Round 16: 1BLdc in every st.

Round 17: 1dc in every st.

Stuff work.

Round 18: [Dc2tog] 6 times (6 sts).

Fasten off and sew opening closed. Embroider the pencil tip using Black. Using Black, add French knots for eyes on round 9, 2 sts apart, and a curved line for the mouth.

Travel

For holiday dreamers, backpackers and gap-year goers, or anyone who wants to have that beach-break feeling without the hassle of a budget airline. Enjoy your own little adventure with a tiny camera, suitcase and even flip flops, or combine with elements from other chapters such as Sealife or About Town to create your own scenery. The little characters are super cute and would give anyone a little holiday cheer.

This chapter uses Scheepjes Sweet Treat cotton threads and a 1.25mm (9/4 steel) hook, but you can go smaller to make your pieces extra travel-sized, or bigger if you have more room in your suitcase!

RUBBER RING

Materials

- 1.25mm-1.5mm (9/4 to 8/7/2 steel) crochet hook (1.5mm hook will produce slightly larger item)
- Scheepjes Sweet Treat in Royal Orange 189, Candle Light 101, Spring Green 513, Yellow Gold 208, Tyrian Purple 128
- Embroidery needle
- 2mm black eye beads
- Gutermann hand quilting cotton in Black 5201 for sewing and embroidery

Finished Size

10mm x 25mm x 25mm (²⁵⁄₆₄in x ⁶³⁄₆₄in x ⁶³⁄₆₄in)

Using Royal Orange, make 10ch, ss in first ch to join.

Round 1 (RS): 1ch (does not count as a st throughout), 1dc in every ch, ss to join (10 sts).

Round 2: 1ch, 2dc in every st, ss to join (20 sts).

Round 3: 1ch, [1dc, 2dc in next st] 10 times, ss to join (30 sts).

Round 4: Using Candle Light and starting in first foundation ch with RS facing, 1ch, 1dc in every st, ss to join (10 sts).

Round 5: 2dc in every st, ss to join (20 sts).

Push Candle Light side through centre ring to make the doughnut.

Round 6: On Candle Light side, work 1ch, [1dc, 2dc in next st] 10 times, ss to join (30 sts).

Round 7: 1ch, 1dc in every st, ss to join.

Round 8: Using Royal Orange, surface ss into the BLs of round 3 together with BLs of round 7 to join, stuffing as you go. Fasten off.

Using Spring Green, Yellow Gold and Tyrian Purple, embroider dots onto the orange side of the ring, leaving enough space for the eyes. Sew eye beads to round 3, 3 stitches apart. Make a little 'V' in between using Black for the smile.

Sew the eye beads onto your finished piece, then use the remaining thread to embroider a tiny smile.

PINEAPPLE

Materials

- 1.25mm-1.5mm (9/4 to 8/7/2 steel) crochet hook (1.5mm hook will produce slightly larger item)
- Scheepjes Sweet Treat in Yellow Gold 208, Spring Green 513
- Embroidery needle
- 2mm black eye beads
- Gutermann hand quilting cotton in Black 5201 for sewing and embroidery

Finished Size

30mm x 12mm x 12mm (1³⁄₁₆in x 1⁵⁄₃₂in x 1⁵⁄₃₂in)

Leaves

Using Spring Green work [7ch, ss in first ch] 3 times, [10ch, ss in first ch] 3 times (6 loops).

Fasten off. Starting at the end with the larger loops, roll up at the base, so the larger loops are in the centre and the smaller loops are around the outside. Use thread ends to secure at the base with a few sts.

Body

Work in continuous rounds, starting with a magic ring in Yellow Gold.

Round 1: 6dc into ring (6 sts).

Round 2: 2dc in every st (12 sts).

Round 3: [3dc, 2dc in next st] 3 times (15 sts).

Rounds 4 to 7: 1dc in every st.

Round 8: [3dc, dc2tog] 3 times (12 sts).

Round 9: [2dc, dc2tog] 3 times (9 sts).

Fasten off and stuff work, weave thread ends around FLs of round 9 like a drawstring bag. Insert the base of leaves into the opening. Pull round 9 thread end, trapping leaves and closing opening. Secure into place with a few sts through the opening and leaf base. Sew eyes on round 5, 3 sts apart. Embroider a little 'V' shape in between using Black for the smile.

PALM TREE

Materials

- 1.25mm-1.5mm (9/4 to 8/7/2 steel) crochet hook (1.5mm hook will produce slightly larger item)
- Scheepjes Sweet Treat in Rust 388, Sage Green 212, Ginger Gold 383, Black Coffee 162
- Embroidery needle
- 2mm black eye beads
- Gutermann hand quilting cotton in Black 5201 for sewing and embroidery
- Pipe cleaner

Finished Size

17mm x 27mm x 17mm (⁴³⁄₆₄in x 1¹⁄₁₆in x ⁴³⁄₆₄in)

Trunk

Work in continuous rounds, starting with a magic ring in Rust.

Round 1: 6dc into ring (6 sts).

Round 2: 2dc in every st (12 sts).

Round 3: 1BLdc in every st.

Rounds 4 to 5: 1dc in every st.

Add a small amount of stuffing.

Round 6: [2dc, dc2tog] 3 times (9 sts).

Rounds 7 to 9: 1dc in every st.

Round 10: [1dc, dc2tog] 3 times (6 sts).

Rounds 11 and 12: 1dc in every st.

Fasten off. Insert a pipe cleaner into trunk and trim to size. Bend any sharp ends over using pliers.

Palm Leaves

Using Sage Green, *make 10ch, starting in second ch from hook and working in the back bumps of the 9 ch, work 1ss, 1dc, 1htr, 1tr, 1htr, 1dc, 1dc, 1ss, 1ss, rep from * 4 more times, ss into base of first leaf to make a star shape. Fasten off and sew thread ends to the top of tree trunk.

Sand Base

Round 1: Using Ginger Gold, starting in any FL of round 3 of the trunk, and working in continuous rounds, work [1dc, 2dc in next st] 6 times (18 sts).

Round 2: 1dc, [1htr, 1tr] in next st, [1tr, 1htr] in next st, 1dc, [1htr, 1tr] in next st, 1tr, [1tr, 1htr] in next st, 2dc, [1htr, 1tr] in next st, 2tr, [1tr, 1htr] in next st, 2dc, [1htr, 1tr] in next st, [1tr, 1htr] in next st, 1dc (26 sts).

Round 3: 1BLss in every st, invisible ss to finish (see Crochet Techniques). Fasten off.

Coconut (make 2)

Using Black Coffee, make a magic ring, into ring work 3ch, tr2tog (makes small bobble), 3ch, tr2tog in bobble just made, fold in half and ss in magic ring to make a little puff ball. Sew one to the underside of the palm leaves and one at the base of the trunk. Sew eye beads on round 4 of trunk, 3 sts apart. Sew a little 'V' shape in between using Black for the smile.

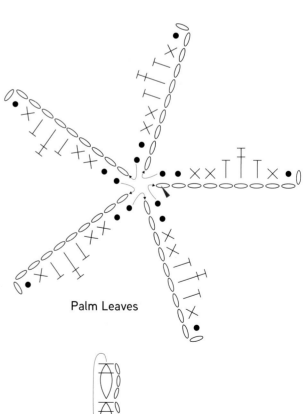

Palm Leaves

Coconut

FLIP FLOPS

Materials

- 1.25mm-1.5mm (9/4 to 8/7/2 steel) crochet hook (1.5mm hook will produce slightly larger item)
- Scheepjes Sweet Treat in Watermelon 252, Spring Green 513
- Embroidery needle

Finished Size

23mm x 14mm x 5mm ($^{29}/_{32}$in x $^{35}/_{64}$in x $^{13}/_{64}$in)

Right Foot (make 2)

Make 2 of each foot, the second ones will make the underside of the second flip flop.

Using Watermelon, make 7ch.

Round 1: Starting in second ch from hook, 1dc in 5 ch, 3dc in next ch, working down other side of foundation ch, 1dc in next 4 ch, 2dc in last ch, do not join round (14 sts).

Round 2: 5dc, 2htr in next st, 3dtr in next st, [2tr, 1htr] in next st, 1dc, invisible ss (see Crochet Techniques).

Left Foot (make 2)

Using Watermelon, make 7ch.

Round 1: Starting in second ch from hook, 3dc in first ch, 1dc in next 4 ch, 3dc in last ch, working down other side of foundation ch, 1dc in next 4 ch (14 sts).

Round 2: [1htr, 2tr] in next st, 3dtr in next st, 2htr in next st, 5dc, invisible ss in next st.

Straps (make 4)

Using Spring Green, make 5ch, fasten off. Use thread ends to sew 2 straps to 1 left and 1 right flip flop. Sew toe ends to the base of 3tr stitches and the other ends to each side.

Take 1 foot with straps and 1 foot without. Place WS together so that the ends from the straps are sandwiched and hidden in between. Using Spring Green and starting on any dtr st, BLss in each pair of sts to join, invisible ss to finish round.

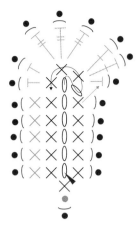

Left Foot

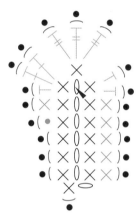

Right Foot

SUITCASE

Materials

- 1.25mm-1.5mm (9/4 to 8/7/2 steel) crochet hook (1.5mm hook will produce slightly larger item)
- Scheepjes Sweet Treat in Moon Rock 254, Black Coffee 162, Bluebird 247, Ginger Gold 383, Rust 388
- Embroidery needle
- 2mm black eye beads
- Gutermann hand quilting cotton in Black 5201 for sewing and embroidery

Finished Size

22mm x 25mm x 15mm ($^{55}⁄_{64}$in x $^{63}⁄_{64}$in x $^{19}⁄_{32}$in)

Body (make 2)

Using Moon Rock, make 8ch.

Rows 1 to 6: 1ch (does not count as a st throughout), turn, 1dc in every st (8 sts).

Mark the second and seventh foundation ch for adding straps later. This also marks the bottom of the suitcase.

Round 7: Do not turn, 1ch, 1dc in the side of st just made, 5dc down short side of rectangle, 2dc in corner ch, 1dc in next 6 ch of foundation row, 2dc in corner ch, 6dc up short side of rectangle, finishing on top left corner (22 sts).

Round 8: 1BLdc in every st, ss to join (30 sts).

Round 9: Using Black Coffee, surface ss in the FLs of round 7 to reinforce edge, invisible ss to join (see Crochet Techniques).

Straps (make 2)

Using Black Coffee, surface crochet 8 sts from one marked foundation ch to the top of the edging, make 6ch for handle, surface crochet back down to the other marked stitch of foundation row. Fasten off and sew in ends.

Using Bluebird, Rust and Ginger Gold, embroider luggage labels where desired, leaving space for the face.

On one side of the suitcase, attach eye beads onto the straps at row 2. Make a little 'V' shape between the eyes for a smile in Black. Using Moon Rock, whipstitch the BLs of both sides to join, stuffing as you go.

Sew the eye beads onto your finished piece, then use the remaining thread to embroider a tiny smile.

CAMERA

Materials

- 1.25mm-1.5mm (9/4 to 8/7/2 steel) crochet hook (1.5mm hook will produce slightly larger item)
- Scheepjes Sweet Treat in Amethyst 240, Tyrian Purple 128, Bridal White 105, Royal Orange 189
- Embroidery needle
- 2mm black eye beads
- Gutermann hand quilting cotton in Black 5201 for sewing and embroidery

Finished Size

17mm x 20mm x 10mm ($^{43}⁄_{64}$in x $^{25}⁄_{32}$in x $^{25}⁄_{64}$in)

Body

Using Tyrian Purple, make 9ch.

Round 1: Starting in second ch from hook, 1dc in 7 ch, 2dc in last ch, working along other side of foundation ch, 1dc in next 7 ch, ss to join (16 sts).

Round 2: 1BLss in every st, invisible ss to finish (see Crochet Techniques).

Join Amethyst in fifth st of round 2.

Round 3: 1dc in BLs of round 1 and BLs of ss of round 2 together in every st, ss to join (16 sts).

Rounds 4 to 6: 1ch (does not count as a st), 1dc in every st, ss to join (16 sts).

Change back to Tyrian Purple.

Round 7: 1BLss in every st.

Round 8: 1dc in BLs of round 6 and BLs of ss in round 7 together in every st (16 sts).

Fasten off, stuff and sew BLs to close opening.

Lens

Round 1: Using Bridal White, make a magic ring, 6dc into ring, invisible ss (see Crochet Techniques) into first st to join (6 sts).

Round 2: Using Tyrian Purple, 1BLss in every st, invisible ss into first st to join.

Sew the lens onto the camera body, covering the ends of rounds. Using Royal Orange embroider a little rectangle on the top right corner for the flash. Use Black to embroider a button to the top of the camera on the opposite side. Sew the eye beads onto your finished piece, then use the remaining thread to embroider a tiny smile.

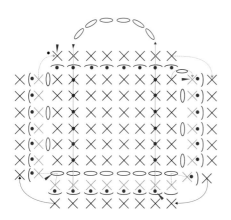

Suitcase

HOT AIR BALLOON

Materials

- 1.25mm-1.5mm (9/4 to 8/7/2 steel) crochet hook (1.5mm hook will produce slightly larger item)
- Scheepjes Sweet Treat in Bluebird (B) 247, Colonial Rose (CR) 398, Tyrian Purple 128
- Embroidery needle
- 2mm black eye beads
- Gutermann hand quilting cotton in Black 5201 for sewing and embroidery

Finished Size

17mm x 27mm x 17mm (⁴³⁄₆₄in x 1¹⁄₁₆in x ⁴³⁄₆₄in)

Balloon

Round 1: Using B, make a magic ring, 6dc into ring, ss to join (6 sts).

Round 2: 1ch in B (does not count as a st throughout), [1dc in B, 1dc in CR] 6 times (12 sts).

Round 3: 1ch in B, [2dc in B in next st, 2dc in CR in next st] 6 times (24 sts).

Rounds 4 to 7: 1ch in B, [2dc in B, 2dc in CR] 6 times.

Round 8: 1ch in B, [dc2tog in B, 2dc in CR] 6 times (18 sts).

Round 9: 1ch in B, [1dc in B, 2dc in CR] 6 times.

Round 10: 1ch in B, [1dc in B, dc2tog in CR] 6 times (12 sts). Stuff work.

Round 11: 1ch in B, [1dc in B, 1dc in CR] 6 times.

Round 12: 1ch in B, 1dc in B in every st.

Fasten off, add further stuffing and sew opening together through the BLs of round 12.

Basket

Round 1: Using Tyrian Purple, ss in any FL of round 12 of the basket, 3ch (counts as 1dc and 2ch), *skip 2 sts, 1FLdc, 2ch, rep from * twice, skip last 2 sts, ss in top of beg 3ch to join (4 hanging ropes).

Round 2: 1ch, 2dc in each 4ch sp, ss to first st to join (8 sts).

Fasten off, use tail end to sew opening together using the BLs only. Sew the eye beads onto your finished piece, then use the remaining thread to embroider a tiny smile.

Aeroplane Tail Fin

Propeller

AEROPLANE

Materials

- 1.25mm-1.5mm (9/4 to 8/7/2 steel) crochet hook (1.5mm hook will produce slightly larger item)
- Scheepjes Sweet Treat in Bluebird 247, Tyrian Purple 128, Bridal White 105
- Embroidery needle
- 2mm black eye beads
- Gutermann hand quilting cotton in Black 5201 for sewing and embroidery

Finished Size

15mm x 40mm x 30mm (1⁹⁄₃₂in x 1³⁷⁄₆₄in x 1³⁄₁₆in)

Main Body

Work in continuous rounds, starting with a magic ring in Bluebird.

Round 1: 6dc into ring (6 sts).

Round 2: 2dc in every st (12 sts).

Round 3: 1dc in every st,

Round 4: [2dc in next st, 3dc] 3 times (15 sts).

Round 5: 1dc in every st.

Round 6: [Dc2tog, 3dc] 3 times (12 sts).

Round 7: 1dc in every st.

Stuff work.

Round 8: [Dc2tog, 2dc] 3 times (9 sts).

Round 9: 1dc in every st.

Round 10: [Dc2tog, 1dc] 3 times (6 sts).

Fasten off and sew closed.

Wing (make 2)

Work in continuous rounds, starting with a magic ring in Tyrian Purple.

Round 1: 6dc into ring (6 sts).

Round 2: [2dc in next st, 2dc] twice (8 sts).

Rounds 3 to 6: 1dc in every st.

Round 7: [2dc in next st, 3dc] twice (10 sts).

Flatten opening so that the 2dc in one st from round 7 are on the corners, sew flat, then sew onto the sides of the plane on rounds 5 to 8.

Tail Fin (make 2 in Tyrian Purple, 1 in Bluebird)

Special stitches: 3trCL – 3 treble st cluster (see Crochet Techniques)

Make a magic ring, into the ring work 3ch, 3trCL, 3ch, 3trCL in top of cluster just made, fasten off and fold in the middle. Use the tail ends to sew the ends of the tail fin together. Attach the Bluebird fin in the middle sticking up, and the 2 Tyrian Purple fins on each side.

Cockpit

Round 1: Using Bridal White, make a magic ring, 8dc into ring, ss to join (8 sts).

Round 2: 1ch (does not count as a st throughout), 8dc, ss to join.

Fasten off and use tail end to sew onto top of aeroplane, between the wings.

Propeller

Using Bridal White, make 2ch, [2dc, 1ch, ss] in second ch from hook, 3ch, [2dc, 1ch, ss] in second ch from hook. Fasten off and sew tail ends to the middle ch and sew to the magic ring of the aeroplane body.

Sew the eye beads onto your finished piece, then use the remaining thread to embroider a tiny smile.

HELICOPTER

Materials

- 1.25mm-1.5mm (9/4 to 8/7/2 steel) crochet hook (1.5mm hook will produce slightly larger item)
- Scheepjes Sweet Treat in Sage Green 212, Bridal White 105, Amethyst 240
- Embroidery needle
- 2mm black eye beads
- Gutermann hand quilting cotton in Black 5201 for sewing and embroidery

Finished Size

20mm x 16mm x 30mm (²⁵⁄₃₂in x ⅝in x 1³⁄₁₆in)

Body

Work in continuous rounds, starting with a magic ring in Bridal White.

Round 1: 6dc into ring (6 sts).

Round 2: 2dc in every st (12 sts).

Change to Amethyst.

Round 3: 1BLss in every st (12 sts).

Round 4: [2dc, 2dc in next st] 4 times in every BL of round 2 and BL of each ss of round 3 together (16 sts).

Round 5: 1dc in every st.

Round 6: [Dc2tog, 6dc] twice (14 sts).

Round 7: 1dc in every st.

Round 8: Dc2tog, 10dc, dc2tog (12 sts).

Round 9: Dc2tog, 8dc, dc2tog (10 sts).

Round 10: Dc2tog, 6dc, dc2tog (8 sts).

Rounds 11 and 12: 1dc in every st.

Fasten off, stuff work and sew opening closed.

Foot (make 2)

Using Amethyst, make a magic ring, work [4ch, dtr4tog] in magic ring, fasten off and pull magic ring closed. Use the ends to sew on the underside of the helicopter.

Blades

Using Sage Green, make a magic ring, 1ch, *1dc, 5ch, starting in second ch from hook, 1htr in next 2 ch, 1dc in next ch, ss in last ch, ss in base dc, rep from * twice more, ss in first base dc st to join. Fasten off.

Blade Topper

Using Amethyst, make a magic ring, 6dc into ring, invisible ss to join (see Crochet Techniques). Use tail ends to sew onto the centre of the blades, then onto the top of the helicopter.

Window (make 2)

Using Bridal White make a magic ring, 6dc into ring, invisible ss to join. Sew windows to the side of the helicopter, sew the propeller to the side of the tail end of body.

Back Propeller

Using Sage Green make a magic ring, 6dc into ring, invisible ss to join.

Sew eye beads to the edge of the front window. Make a little 'V' shape using Black on the magic ring for the smile.

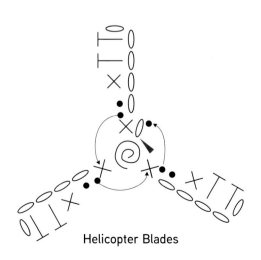

Helicopter Blades

BOAT

Materials

- 1.25mm-1.5mm (9/4 to 8/7/2 steel) crochet hook (1.5mm hook will produce slightly larger item)
- Scheepjes Sweet Treat in Bluebird 247, Bridal White 105, Ginger Gold 383, Red 722
- Embroidery needle
- 2mm black eye beads
- Gutermann hand quilting cotton in Black 5201 for sewing and embroidery

Finished Size

20mm x 20mm x 25mm (²⁵⁄₃₂in x ²⁵⁄₃₂in x ⁶³⁄₆₄in)

Cabin

Work in continuous rounds, starting with a magic ring in Bluebird.

Round 1: 8dc into ring (8 sts).

Round 2: [1dc, 2dc in next st] 4 times (12 sts).

Change to Bridal White.

Round 3: 1BLss in any st to start, 1BLdc in every st, ss to join (12 sts).

Rounds 4 to 7: 1ch (does not count as a st throughout), 12dc, ss to join.

Fasten off, leaving long tail for sewing, stuff but do not sew closed.

Deck

Round 1: Using Ginger Gold, make a magic ring, 1ch, 8dc into ring, ss to join (8 sts).

Round 2: 1ch (does not count as a st throughout), 3dc, 3dc in next st, 1dc, 3dc in next st, 2dc, 1dc in first st of prev round, ss to join (13 sts).

Round 3: 1ch, 2dc in first st, 4dc, 3dc in next st, 1dc, 3dc in next st, 4dc, 2dc in last st, ss to join (19 sts).

Round 4: 1ch, 2dc in first st, 6dc, 3dc in next st, 3dc, 3dc in next st, 6dc, 2dc in last st, ss to join (25 sts).

Fasten off and sew the cabin to the wider portion of the deck.

Hull and Base

Using Red, rep rounds 1 to 4 of deck to make the base.

Round 5: 1ch, 1BLdc in every st, ss to join (25 sts).

Round 6: 1ch, 1dc in every st.

Add some stuffing, place the deck inside the hull base and line up the outer stitches, ready for joining.

Round 7: Ss the BLs of hull round 6 and BLs of deck round 4 together, add more stuffing if needed.

Round 8: (1ch, ss) in each st, ss to join.

Fasten off and sew in ends. Using Bridal White embroider a small anchor to the front of the boat. Sew eye beads to the cabin on round 6, 4 stitches apart. Embroider mouth using Black.

Boat Hull and Base

Space

Explore the great unknown from the pillowy confines of your craft corner, complete with blanket, your favourite TV show, crochet hook and hot beverage. Fantastic compromise in my opinion, it's raining outside anyway…

The amis in this chapter are crocheted with Scheepjes Sweet Treat cotton threads and a 1.25mm (9/4 steel) hook. On a couple of the planets you will need to change colour mid-round – check out how to do this in the Techniques section.

SUN

Materials

- 1.25mm-1.5mm (9/4 to 8/7/2 steel) crochet hook (1.5mm hook will produce slightly larger item)
- Scheepjes Sweet Treat in Yellow Gold 208, Watermelon 252
- Embroidery needle
- 2mm black eye beads and cotton thread for sewing

Finished Size

20mm x 20mm x 10mm ($^{25}/_{32}$in x $^{25}/_{32}$in x $^{25}/_{64}$in)

Body (make 2)

Work in continuous rounds, starting with a magic ring in Yellow Gold.

Round 1: 6dc into ring (6 sts).

Round 2: 2dc in every st (12 sts).

Round 3: [2dc in next st, 1dc] 6 times (18 sts).

Round 4: 1dc in every st, 1BLss in next st before fastening off.

Using tail ends to stuff work, crochet into the FLs of each half to join as you go.

Flare

Round 5: Using Watermelon, 1FLss in any st, [1ch, (1FLdc, 2ch, 1FLdc) in next st, 1ch, ss in next st] 9 times, stuffing as you go, ending before last ss, fasten off and sew end to first st of round for less visible end of round.

Attach the eye beads on opposite sides of round 3, with the magic ring between the eyes. Embroider a mouth between the eyes using Black.

STAR

Materials

- 1.25mm-1.5mm (9/4 to 8/7/2 steel) crochet hook for large star (1.5mm hook will produce slightly larger item)
- 0.75mm-0.9mm (14/10 to 14/8 steel) crochet hook for small star (0.9mm will produce slightly larger item)
- Scheepjes Sweet Treat in Yellow Gold 208 (large star); Gütermann top stitching thread in Pale Pink 758 (small star)
- Embroidery needle
- 2mm black eye beads and cotton thread for sewing

Finished Size

Large, 25mm x 25mm x 10mm ($^{63}/_{64}$in x $^{63}/_{64}$in x $^{25}/_{64}$in)

Small, 17mm x 17mm x 6mm ($^{43}/_{64}$in x $^{43}/_{64}$in x $^{15}/_{64}$in)

Body (make 2)

Round 1: Using chosen colour and hook size, make a magic ring, 5dc into ring (5 sts).

Round 2: [1dc, 4ch, starting in second ch from hook, 1dc in next 3 ch, 1dc in first st of same round] 4 times, 1dc, 4ch, starting in second ch from hook, 1dc in next 3 ch, dc2tog over last st of round 1 and first st of this round (5 points for star).

Round 3: [1dc in next 2 ch towards star point, 2dc in third ch at star point (turns corner), 1dc in next 3dc on other side of star point, dc2tog over next 2 dc] 4 times, 1dc in next 2 ch towards star point, 2dc in third ch at star point (turns corner), 1dc in next 3dc on other side of star point, ss in dc2tog from end of round 2. Fasten off.

Whipstitch the BLs of the two halves together to join, stuffing as you go. Sew on eye beads and embroider a 'V' shape just above the magic ring in black for a smile.

Sun Body & Flare

Star Body

CLOUD

Materials

- 1.25mm-1.5mm (9/4 to 8/7/2 steel) crochet hook (1.5mm hook will produce slightly larger item)
- Scheepjes Sweet Treat in Bridal White 105
- Embroidery needle
- 2mm black eye beads
- Gutermann hand quilting cotton in Black 5201 for sewing and embroidery

Finished Size

15mm x 30mm x 12mm ($^{19}/_{32}$in x $1^3/_{16}$in x $^{15}/_{32}$in)

Work in continuous rounds, starting with a magic ring in Bridal White.

Round 1: 6dc into ring (6 sts).

Round 2: 2dc in every st (12 sts).

Round 3: [2dc in next st, 3dc] 3 times (15 sts).

Round 4: [Dc2tog] 3 times, 9dc (12 sts).

Round 5: 2dc in first st, 3dc in next st, 2dc in next st, 9dc (16 sts).

Round 6: 2dc, 2dc in next 3 sts, 11dc (19 sts).

Rounds 7 to 9: 1dc in every st.

Round 10: 2dc, [dc2tog] 3 times, 11dc (16 sts).

Round 11: Dc2tog, dc3tog, dc2tog, 9dc (12 sts).

Stuff work.

Round 12: [2dc in next st, 3dc] 3 times (15 sts).

Round 13: 1dc in every st.

Round 14: [Dc2tog, 3dc] 3 times (12 sts).

Round 15: [Dc2tog] 6 times (6 sts).

Fasten off and sew in ends. Attach eye beads in line with the beginning and end of the centre bump, embroider mouth between eyes in black.

MOON

Materials

- 1.25mm-1.5mm (9/4 to 8/7/2 steel) crochet hook for large moon (1.5mm hook will produce slightly larger item)
- 0.75mm-0.9mm (14/10 to 14/8 steel) crochet hook for small moon (0.9mm will produce slightly larger item)
- Scheepjes Sweet Treat in Candle Light 101 (large moon); Gütermann top stitching thread in Pale Blue 75 (small moon)
- Embroidery needle
- 2mm black eye beads
- Gutermann hand quilting cotton in Black 5201 for sewing and embroiderY

Finished Size

Large, 22mm x 22mm x 8mm ($^{55}/_{64}$in x $^{55}/_{64}$in x $^5/_{16}$in)

Small, 14mm x 14mm x 5mm ($^{35}/_{64}$in x $^{35}/_{64}$in x $1^3/_{64}$in)

Work in continuous rounds, starting with a magic ring using chosen colour and hook size.

Round 1: 6dc into ring (6 sts).

Round 2: 3dc in every st (18 sts).

Round 3: 2dc in every st (36 sts).

Round 4: 2dc in next 3 sts, 12dc, 2dc in next 6 sts, 12dc, 2dc in next 3 sts (48 sts).

Fasten off, leave long tail for sewing. Fold in half, whipstitch FLs of both sides together to join, stuffing as you go. Attach eye beads, embroider 'V' shaped mouth along inner edge in Black.

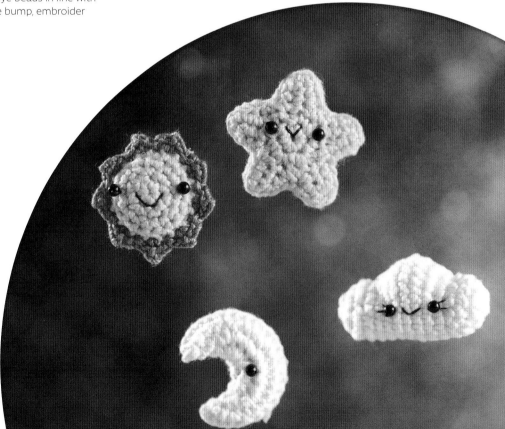

ASTRONAUT

Materials

- 1.25mm-1.5mm (9/4 to 8/7/2 steel) crochet hook (1.5mm hook will produce slightly larger item)
- Scheepjes Sweet Treat in Bridal White 105, Jet Black 110, Moon Rock 254, Hot Red 115, Yellow Gold 208, Watermelon 252
- Embroidery needle

Finished Size

25mm x 20mm x 20mm (⁶³⁄₆₄in x ²⁵⁄₃₂in x ²⁵⁄₃₂in)

Body

Special stitches: bobble - 4 treble st bobble (see Crochet Techniques)

Using Bridal White, make 6ch.

Round 1: Starting in second ch from hook, [1dc, 2dc in next st] twice, 4dc in last ch, working on other side of foundation ch, [2dc in next st, 1dc] twice, 2dc in beg ch (18 sts).

Round 2: 1bobble (see Crochet Techniques), 5dc, 1bobble, 11dc (16dc, 2 bobbles for legs).

Rounds 3 to 4: 1dc in every st.

Round 5: 1dc, 1bobble, 5dc, 1bobble, 10dc (16 dc, 2 bobbles for arms).

Rounds 6 to 11: 1dc in every st.

Round 12: [Dc2tog, 1dc] 6 times (12 sts). Stuff work.

Round 13: [Dc2tog] 6 times (6 sts). Fasten off and sew in ends.

Visor

Work in continuous rounds, starting with a magic ring in Jet Black.

Round 1: 6dc into ring (6 sts).

Round 2: [3dc in next 2 sts, 1dc] twice (14 sts).

Round 3: 1BLss in every st, fasten off with invisible ss (14 sts).

Round 4: change to Bridal White, ss in BL of each st in round 2, behind sts of round 3 (14 sts).

Fasten off with invisible ss and use tail ends to sew 2 small dashes onto the top left side of the visor, then sew onto the body.

Ear Protector (make 2)

Using Bridal White, make a magic ring.

Round 1: 10dc into ring, invisible ss to join (see Crochet Techniques), fasten off. Use Hot Red to embroider a little dash from the magic ring to any one of the 10 sts, sew onto the sides of the head.

Using Watermelon, sew a running stitch around the tummy between rows 3 and 4, this needs to be done before adding the backpack control panel. Using Yellow Gold, Watermelon and Hot Red, sew 3 little dashes above the line to make buttons.

Backpack Control Panel

Using Moon Rock, make 5ch.

Rows 1 to 12: 1ch (does not count as a stitch), turn, 5dc (5 sts).

Fasten off leaving long ends for sewing. Embroider buttons in Bridal White, Hot Red and Watermelon to the top half of the strip. Fold in half, sew the sides together using Moon Rock. The top opening can also be sewn shut or left open to make a little pocket. Sew to the back of the body.

ALIEN

Materials

- 1.25mm-1.5mm (9/4 to 8/7/2 steel) crochet hook`(1.5mm hook will produce slightly larger item)
- Scheepjes Sweet Treat in Sage Green 212
- Embroidery needle
- 2mm black eye beads and cotton thread for sewing

Finished Size

30mm x 16mm x 16mm (1³⁄₁₆in x ⅝in x ⅝in)

Antennae (make 2)

Using Sage Green make a loose slip knot and place onto hook as normal, 1ch, [2dc, 1ch, ss] into the slip knot, use tail end of slip knot to make 4PCIC (see Crochet Techniques). Fasten off.

Body

Work in continuous rounds, starting with a magic ring in Sage Green.

Round 1: 6dc into ring (6 sts).

Round 2: 2dc in every st (12 sts).

Round 3: [2dc in next st, 1dc] 6 times (18 sts).

Use tail ends to sew antennae to top of alien.

Rounds 4 to 10: 1dc in every st.

Round 11: Working in FLs only, [3htr in next st, ss in next 2 sts] 6 times (6 legs).

Stuff work.

Round 12: Work in BLs of round 10 only [BLdc2tog, 1dc] 6 times (12 sts).

Round 13: [Dc2tog] 6 times (6 sts).

Fasten off and sew in ends. Attach eye beads on round 4, embroider mouth using Black between eyes.

ROCKET

Materials

- 1.25mm-1.5mm (9/4 to 8/7/2 steel) crochet hook (1.5mm hook will produce slightly larger item)
- Scheepjes Sweet Treat in Vivid Blue 146, Bridal White 105, Hot Red 115 , Moon Rock 254
- Embroidery needle

Finished Size

30mm x 20mm x 20mm (1³⁄₁₆in x ²⁵⁄₃₂in x ²⁵⁄₃₂in)

Body

Round 1: Starting with a magic ring in Hot Red, 6dc into ring, ss to join (6 sts).

Round 2: 1ch (does not count as a st throughout), [2dc in next st, 1dc] 3 times, ss to join (9 sts).

Round 3: 1ch, [2dc in next st, 2dc] 3 times, ss to join (12 sts).

Change to Bridal White, work in continuous rounds.

Round 4: [2BLdc in next st, 3BLdc] 3 times (15 sts).

Round 5: 1dc in every st.

Round 6: [2dc in next st, 4dc] 3 times (18 sts).

Round 7: 1dc in every st.

Round 8: [Dc2tog, 4dc] 3 times (15 sts).

Round 9: [Dc2tog, 3dc] 3 times (12 sts).

Change to Moon Rock.

Round 10: 1BLss in any st, 1ch, 1dc in every st, ss to join (12 sts).

Round 11: 1ch, 1dc in every st, ss to join.

Stuff work, fasten off and sew to close through BLs of round 10.

Fin (make 3)

Using Hot Red, ss into first FL in round 9, 3ch, 4dtrBO in same FL, 3ch, 4dtrBO on top of bobble just made. Fasten off. Fold back on itself and use tail end of second bobble to join to base of the first bobble. Secure into position by adding a few stitches to both sides of the bobble. Add two more fins in the same way, 3 sts apart from each other.

Window

Using Vivid Blue, make a magic ring, 7dc into ring, ss to first st to join. Fasten off and sew to main body of rocket, between 2 fins.

Rocket Fin

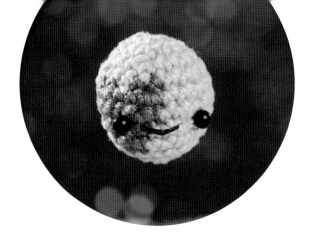

RINGED PLANET

Materials

- 1.25mm-1.5mm (9/4 to 8/7/2 steel) crochet hook (1.5mm hook will produce slightly larger item)
- Scheepjes Sweet Treat in Colonial Rose 398, Spring Green 513, Cherry 413
- Embroidery needle
- 2mm black eye beads
- Gutermann hand quilting cotton in Black 5201 for sewing and embroidery

Finished Size

18mm x 30mm x 30mm ($^{45}\!/_{64}$in x 1$^3\!/_{16}$in x 1$^3\!/_{16}$in)

Body (make 2)

Work in continuous rounds, starting with a magic ring in Colonial Rose.

Round 1: 6dc into ring (6 sts).

Round 2: 2dc in every st (12 sts).

Round 3: [2dc in next st, 1dc] 6 times (15 sts).

Round 4: [2dc in next st, 4dc] 3 times (18 sts).

Round 5: 1dc in every st.

Ss in BL of next st to finish, fasten off and sew in ends. Change to Spring Green to join the 2 halves together.

Round 6: Ss together through BLs of one st of each half, [2dc in next pair of BLs, 1dc in next pair of BLs] 9 times, joining and stuffing as you go, ss to finish (27 sts).

Round 7: 1ch (does not count as a st), 1dc in every st, ss to finish.

Round 8: Change to Cherry, ss in first st, 1back-dc (crab st) in every st.

Fasten off and sew in ends. Sew eye beads 5 sts apart on round 4 of the top half of the planet. Embroider mouth using Black between eyes.

HEART PLANET

Materials

- 1.25mm-1.5mm (9/4 to 8/7/2 steel) crochet hook (1.5mm hook will produce slightly larger item)
- Scheepjes Sweet Treat in Royal Orange (O) 189, Spring Green (G) 513
- Embroidery needle
- 2mm black eye beads
- Gutermann hand quilting cotton in Black 5201 for sewing and embroidery

Finished Size

18mm x 18mm x 18mm ($^{45}\!/_{64}$in x $^{45}\!/_{64}$in x $^{45}\!/_{64}$in)

This pattern uses increases and decreases in unexpected places around the heart shape to ensure crisp clean edges, the invisible decrease technique was used for this design (see Crochet Techniques). Start at the bottom and work your way up from right to left.

Work in continuous rounds, starting with a magic ring in Spring Green.

Round 1: 6dc into ring (6 sts).

Round 2: 2dc in every st (12 sts).

Round 3: [1dc, 2dc in next st] 6 times (18 sts).

Round 4: 4dc in G, 2dc in O, 1dc in G, 2dc in O, 9 dc in G (4 O, 14 G sts).

Round 5: 2dc in G, 2dc in next st in G, 1dc in G, 1dc in O, 2dc in next st in O, 2dc in O, 2dc in next st in O, [2dc in G, 2dc in next st in G] 3 times (7 O, 17 G sts).

Round 6: 4dc in G, 2dc in next st in G, dc2tog in O, 5dc in O, 12dc in G (6 O, 18 G sts).

Round 7: [Dc2tog in G] twice, 1dc in G, 2dc in next st in G, dc2tog in O, 2dc in O, dc2tog in O, 2dc in next st in G, [dc2tog in G, 1dc in G] 3 times, dc2tog in G (4 O, 14 G sts).

Round 8: 4dc in G, 2dc in next st in G, [dc2tog in O] twice, 2dc in next st in G, 8dc in G (2 O, 16 G sts).

Fasten off O, continue in G only.

Round 9: [1dc, dc2tog] 6 times (12 sts). Stuff work.

Round 10: [Dc2tog] 6 times (6 sts).

Fasten off and sew opening closed. Attach eye beads onto round 6, one in the centre of the heart and the other in the Spring Green area, 4 sts apart. Embroider a little 'V' shape in Black in between the eyes for the smile.

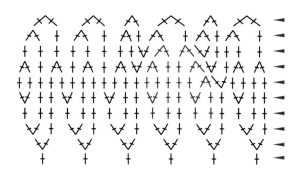

Heart Planet

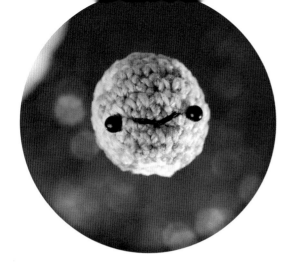

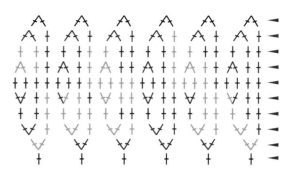

Earth

EARTH

Materials

- 1.25mm-1.5mm (9/4 to 8/7/2 steel) crochet hook (1.5mm hook will produce slightly larger item)
- Scheepjes Sweet Treat in Bridal White 105, Vivid Blue (B) 146, Spring Green (G) 513
- Embroidery needle
- 2mm black eye beads
- Gutermann hand quilting cotton in Black 5201 for sewing and embroidery

Finished Size

18mm x 18mm x 18mm (⁴⁵⁄₆₄in x ⁴⁵⁄₆₄in x ⁴⁵⁄₆₄in)

This pattern involves increasing and decreasing double crochet stitches while changing colour mid row, carrying the yarn using the tapestry technique. Refer to the diagram, start at the bottom and work your way up from right to left.

Work in continuous rounds, starting with a magic ring in Bridal White.

Round 1: 6dc into ring (6 sts).

Change to G.

Round 2: 2dc in next st in G, [2dc in next st in B] 4 times, 2dc in next st in G (8 B, 4 G sts).

Round 3: 1dc in B, 2dc in next st in G, 1dc in G, 2dc in next st in G, 1dc in B, 2dc in next st in B, [1dc in G, 2dc in next st in G] twice, 1dc in G, 2dc in next st in B (6 B, 12 G sts).

Round 4: 2dc in B, 3dc in G, 6dc in B, 5dc in G, 2dc in B (10 B, 8 G sts).

Round 5: 2dc in B, [1dc in B, 1dc in G] all in next st, 2dc in G, 2dc in next st in B, 2dc in B, 2dc in next st in B, 2dc in G, 2dc in next st in G, 1dc in B, 1dc in G, [1dc in G, 1dc in B] all in next st, 1dc in G, 1dc in B, 2dc in next st in B (14 B, 10 G sts).

Round 6: 5dc in B, 4dc in G, 3dc in B, 5dc in G, 7dc in B (15 B, 9 G sts).

Round 7: 2dc in B, dc2tog in B, 1dc in B, 1dc in G, dc2tog in G, 1dc in G, 1dc in B, dc2tog in B, 2dc in B, dc2tog in G, 1dc in G, 1dc in B, dc2tog in B, 1dc in B, 1dc in G, dc2tog in G (11 B, 7 G sts).

Round 8: 5dc in B, 2dc in G, 4dc in B, 2dc in G, 3dc in B, 2dc in G (12 B, 6 G sts).

Round 9: [1dc in B, dc2tog in B] twice, 1dc in G, [dc2tog in B, 1dc in B] 3 times, dc2tog in B (11 B, 1 G sts).

Stuff work. Change to Bridal White.

Round 10: [Dc2tog] 6 times (6 sts).

Fasten off and sew opening closed. Attach eye beads on round 6, one on Brazil and one on central Africa. Embroider a little 'V' shape in Black between the eyes for the smile.

Sealife

Sealife is an amigurumi staple, nothing puts a smile on my face like a pudgy octopus or a tiny whale. This chapter features both of these, as well as a seahorse, a turtle, a dolphin, and others. These little makes are a great gift for someone who needs cheering up, or for any lovers of the deep blue sea.

Once you have conquered those designs in micro-crochet, have a go at making these in chunky or fluffy yarns to create something extra cuddly. Swap around the colours and embroider different markings for extra variety.

TURTLE

Materials

- 1.25mm-1.5mm (9/4 to 8/7/2 steel) crochet hook (1.5mm hook will produce slightly larger item)
- Scheepjes Sweet Treat in Moon Rock 254, Sage Green 212
- Embroidery needle
- 1mm black eye beads and cotton thread for sewing

Finished Size

19mm x 25mm x 25mm (¾in x ⁶³⁄₆₄in x ⁶³⁄₆₄in)

Body

Special stitches: 3trCL – 3 treble cluster stitch (see Crochet Techniques)

Work in continuous rounds, starting with a magic ring in Moon Rock.

Round 1: 6dc into ring (6 sts).

Round 2: 2dc in every st (12 sts).

Round 3: [3dc, 2dc in next st] 3 times (15 sts).

Round 4: [1BLdc, 2ch, 1BLdc] in same st for tail, ss in next st, *[1BLss, 2ch, 1BL3trCL, 2ch, ss in second ch from hook, 2ch, 1BLss] in next st for fin, ss in next st, rep from * for second fin, ss in next 5 sts, **[1BLss, 4ch, ss in second ch from hook, 1BL3trCL, 2ch, 1BLss] in next st for third fin, ss in next st, rep from ** for last fin, ss in first BLdc from tail to join. Fasten off (4 fins, 1 tail, 10 ss).

Change to Sage Green, work in continuous rounds.

Round 5: 1dc in FL from tail, 1dc in next st, 2dc in next FL from fin, 1dc in next st, 2dc in next FL from fin, 1dc in next 6 sts, 2dc in next FL from fin, 1dc in next st, 2dc in last FL from fin, 1dc in next st, 1dc in beg FL from tail (20 sts).

Rounds 6 to 8: 1dc in every st.

Round 9: [3dc, dc2tog] 4 times (16 sts).

Round 10: [2dc, dc2tog] 4 times (12 sts). Stuff work.

Round 11: [Dc2tog] 6 times (6 sts).

Fasten off and sew in ends.

Head

Work in continuous rounds, starting with a magic ring in Moon Rock.

Round 1: 6dc into ring (6 sts).

Round 2: 2dc in every st (12 sts).

Round 3: 1dc in every st.

Round 4: [Dc2tog, 4dc] twice (10 sts).

Fasten off and stuff head, sew to body using the magic ring tail, between the 2 front fins. Attach eye beads on round 2 on either side of magic ring.

YELLOW FISHY

Materials

- 1.25mm-1.5mm (9/4 to 8/7/2 steel) crochet hook (1.5mm hook will produce slightly larger item)
- Scheepjes Sweet Treat in Yellow Gold 208
- Embroidery needle
- 2mm black eye beads and cotton thread for sewing

Finished Size

17mm x 17mm x 23mm (⁴³⁄₆₄in x ⁴³⁄₆₄in x ²⁹⁄₃₂in)

Body

Work in continuous rounds, starting with a magic ring in Yellow Gold.

Round 1: 6dc into ring (6 sts).

Round 2: 2dc in every st (12 sts).

Round 3: [2dc in next st, 2dc] 4 times (16 sts).

Rounds 4 to 5: 1dc in every st.

Round 6: [1FLss, 2ch, 2FLhtr, 2ch, 1FLss] in first st for fin, 8dc, [1FLss, 2ch, 2FLhtr, 2ch, 1FLss] in next st for second fin, 6dc (14 sts, 2 fins).

Round 7: 1dc in every st and the 2 BL sts behind fins (16 sts).

Stuff work and attach eye beads on round 3 on either side of the fish, in line with the base of the fins.

Round 8: [Dc2tog] 8 times (8 sts).

Tail

Flatten opening and join 2 sides of 4 sts together, [ss, 3ch] in first st, [3tr, 3ch, ss] in next st, [ss, 3ch] in next st, [3tr, 3ch, ss] in last st.

Fasten off and sew in ends.

Top Fin

Using Yellow Gold, make a magic ring, [2ch, 2htr] into ring, fasten off. This part is sewn on upside down, the magic ring makes the tip of the fin. Sew the tops of the sts to the body of the fish. Attach eye beads on either side of face.

CRAB

Materials

- 1.25mm-1.5mm (9/4 to 8/7/2 steel) crochet hook (1.5mm hook will produce slightly larger item)
- Scheepjes Sweet Treat in Rust 388
- Embroidery needle
- 2mm black eye beads and cotton thread for sewing

Finished Size

17mm x 25mm x 28mm (4³⁄₆₄in x 6³⁄₆₄in x 1⁷⁄₆₄in)

Body

Special stitches: puff (see Crochet Techniques)

Work in continuous rounds, starting with a magic ring in Rust.

Round 1: 6dc into ring (6 sts).

Round 2: 2dc in every st (12 sts).

Round 3: [(2dc in next st) twice, 4dc] twice (16 sts).

Round 4: 1dc, [2dc in next st] twice, 6dc, [2dc in next st] twice, 5dc (20 sts).

Rounds 5 to 6: 1dc in every st.

Round 7: *[Puff, 1dc] twice, puff, 5dc, rep from * once.

Round 8: 1dc in next 5 sts (including the puffs), dc2tog, 1dc, dc2tog, 1dc in next 5 sts, dc2tog, 1dc, dc2tog (16 sts).

Round 9: [2dc, dc2tog] 4 times (12 sts).

Stuff work.

Round 10: [Dc2tog] 6 times (6 sts).

Sew hole closed and fasten off.

Pincer (make 2)

Round 1: Using Rust make a magic ring, 6dc into ring, ss to join (6 sts).

Round 2: 1ch, [(2dc in next st) twice, 1dc] twice, ss to join (10 sts).

Fold in half, 1ch, BLss together to join first 2 sts, [1BLss, 2ch, 1BLss] in next st, 2BLss, joining as you go, no need to stuff. Fasten off and sew to front of crab. Attach eye beads 3 stitches apart on round 7, just next to the front pincers.

OCTOPUS

Materials

- 1.25mm-1.5mm (9/4 to 8/7/2 steel) crochet hook (1.5mm hook will produce slightly larger item)
- Scheepjes Sweet Treat in Amethyst 240
- Embroidery needle
- 2mm black eye beads and cotton thread for sewing

Finished Size

15mm x 18mm x 18mm (19⁄₃₂in x 45⁄₆₄in x 45⁄₆₄in)

Special stitches: puff (see Crochet Techniques)

Work in continuous rounds, starting with a magic ring in Amethyst.

Round 1: 6dc into ring (6 sts).

Round 2: 2dc in every st (12 sts).

Round 3: [2dc in next st, 1dc] 6 times (18 sts).

Round 4: [2dc in next st, 2dc] 6 times (24 sts).

Rounds 5 to 6: 1dc in every st.

Round 7: [Dc2tog, 2dc] 6 times (18 sts).

Round 8: [Dc2tog, 7dc] twice (16 sts).

Round 9: [(1FLss, 1FLpuff, 1ch, 1FLss) in next st, 1FLss in next st] 8 times, ss in BL of first puff st to join (8 legs).

Stuff work.

Round 10: 1ch (does not count as a st), [BLdc2tog] 8 times (8 sts).

Fasten off and finish stuffing. Attach eye beads on round 8, 4 sts apart. They should be nestled just above the legs and there should be 2 legs between the eyes.

Crab Pincer

DOLPHIN

Materials

- 1.25mm-1.5mm (9/4 to 8/7/2 steel) crochet hook (1.5mm hook will produce slightly larger item)
- Scheepjes Sweet Treat in Vivid Blue 146
- Embroidery needle
- 1mm black eye beads and cotton thread for sewing
- Pipe cleaner or jewellery wire

Finished Size

15mm x 15mm x 43mm (¹⁹⁄₃₂in x ¹⁹⁄₃₂in x 1¹¹⁄₁₆in)

Body

Work in continuous rounds, starting with a magic ring in Vivid Blue.

Round 1: 6dc into ring (6 sts).

Round 2: 1dc in every st (6 sts).

Round 3: 2dc in next st, 2BLdc in each of next 2 sts, 2dc in next st, 2dc (10 sts).

Round 4: 3dc, 2dc in each of next 2 sts, 5dc (12 sts).

Rounds 5 to 8: 1dc in every st.

Round 9: 1dc, [1FLss, 2ch, 1FLtr, 2ch, ss in tr, 2ch, 1FLss] in next st, 8dc, [1FLss, 2ch, 1FLtr, 2ch, ss in tr, 2ch, 1FLss] in next st, 1dc (10 sts, 2 fins).

Round 10: 1dc in every dc and BL of sts behind fins (12 sts).

Round 11: 1dc in every st.

Insert a piece of pipe cleaner or wire, stuffing as you go.

Round 12: 1dc, dc2tog, 6dc, dc2tog, 1dc (10 sts).

Round 13: 1dc in every st.

Round 14: 2dc, dc2tog, 3dc, dc2tog, 1dc (8 sts).

Round 15: [2dc, dc2tog] twice (6 sts).

Fasten off.

Tail Fin (make 2)

Round 1 (RS): Using Vivid Blue make a magic ring, 6dc into ring, ss to join (6 sts).

Round 2: 1ch, 2dc in every st, ss to join (12 sts).

Fold in half WS touching to make a semi-circle shape, 1ch, join using 6BLs along edge. No need for stuffing. Fasten off, leave ends for sewing.

Sew fins together at the corners, with ss edges facing each other, then sew to the back of the dolphin.

Top Fin

Using Vivid Blue, make a magic ring, [2ch, 2htr] into ring, fasten off. This part is sewn on upside down, the magic ring makes the tip of the fin. Sew the tops of the sts to the top of the dolphin between the fins. Attach eye beads on each side of the face.

JELLYFISH

Materials

- 1.25mm-1.5mm (9/4 to 8/7/2 steel) crochet hook (1.5mm hook will produce slightly larger item)
- Scheepjes Sweet Treat in Ruby 517
- Embroidery needle
- 2mm black eye beads and cotton thread for sewing

Finished Size

30mm x 15mm x 15mm (1³⁄₁₆in x ¹⁹⁄₃₂in x ¹⁹⁄₃₂in)

Work in continuous rounds, starting with a magic ring in Ruby.

Round 1: 6dc into ring (6 sts).

Round 2: 2dc in every st (12 sts).

Round 3: [2dc in next st, 1dc] 6 times (18 sts).

Rounds 4 to 5: 1dc in every st.

Round 6: [Dc2tog, 1dc] 6 times (12 sts).

Round 7: [(1FLss, 2FLhtr, 1FLss) in same st, 1FLss in next st] 6 times (12 FLhtr).

Round 8: Working in BLs only, [(1BLss, 13 ch, starting in second ch from hook, 2dc in every ch for corkscrew, 1BLss) all in same st, 1BLdc in next st, BLdc2tog] 3 times.

Fasten off, stuff work and sew opening closed. Attach eye beads 4 sts apart on round 6.

SEAHORSE

Materials

- 1.25mm-1.5mm (9/4 to 8/7/2 steel) crochet hook (1.5mm hook will produce slightly larger item)
- Scheepjes Sweet Treat in Cherry 413, Colonial Rose 398
- Embroidery needle
- 2mm black eye beads and cotton thread for sewing
- Pipe cleaner or jewellery wire (optional)

Finished Size

40mm x 12mm x 20mm (1³⁷⁄₆₄in x ¹⁵⁄₃₂in x ²⁵⁄₃₂in)

Head and Body

Work in continuous rounds, starting with a magic ring in Cherry.

Round 1: 6dc into ring (6 sts).

Round 2: 2dc in every st (12 sts).

Round 3: [2dc in next st, 2dc] 4 times (16 sts).

Round 4: 1dc in every st.

Round 5: [Dc2tog, 2dc] 4 times (12 sts).

Round 6: [Dc2tog, 2dc] 3 times (9 sts).

Head is complete, stuff as you go from this point.

Round 7: 2dc in every st (18 sts).

Rounds 8 to 9: 1dc in every st.

Round 10: Dc2tog, 1dc, dc2tog, 13dc (16 sts).

Round 11: Dc2tog, 1dc, dc2tog, 11dc (14 sts).

Insert wire now if required.

Round 12: Dc2tog, 1dc, dc2tog, 9dc (12 sts).

Round 13: [Dc2tog, 2dc] 3 times (9 sts).

Round 14: [Dc2tog, 1dc] 3 times (6 sts).

Rounds 15 to 25: 1dc in every st.

Fasten off.

Finishing the Tail

Option 1, with wire: trim wire, bend and flatten the end with pliers so that no sharp ends poke through, sew the opening closed. Curl the tail into any position.

Option 2, without wire: little to no stuffing is required for the ends, sew opening closed. Wind into a coil and use a thread end to sew into place.

Crown

Using Colonial Rose make *2ch, (1htr, 1dc) in second ch from hook, rep from * twice more. Fasten off and use ends to sew to top of head.

Fin (make 2)

Using Colonial Rose, make a magic ring, 3ch, 3tr in magic ring, 3ch, ss in magic ring. Fasten off and use ends for sewing onto side of body.

Nose

Using Cherry, make a magic ring, [2ch, 4htr, ss in second ch], fasten off. Pull magic ring tight and pinch out so that it makes a tube shape. The magic ring end makes the tip of the nose. Sew the tops of the htr sts to the head. Attach eye beads to round 4 of the head, on either side of the nose, 4 sts apart.

Seahorse Fin

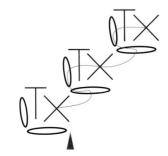

Crown

WHALE

Materials

- 1.25mm-1.5mm (9/4 to 8/7/2 steel) crochet hook (1.5mm hook will produce slightly larger item)
- Scheepjes Sweet Treat in Bluebird 247, Bridal White 105
- Embroidery needle
- 2mm black eye beads and cotton thread for sewing

Finished Size

12mm x 20mm x 23mm (15/32in x 25/32in x 29/32in)

Work in continuous rounds, starting with a magic ring in Bluebird.

Round 1: 6dc into ring (6 sts).

Round 2: 2dc in every st (12 sts).

Round 3: [3dc, 2dc in next st] 3 times (15 sts).

Round 4: [4dc, 2dc in next st] 3 times (18 sts).

Rounds 5 to 6: 1dc in every st.

Round 7: [1FLss, 2ch, 1FLtr, 2ch, 1FLtr, 2ch, 1FLss] in same st for tail, 1dc, dc2tog, 1dc, [1FLss, 2ch, 1FLhtr, 2ch, 1FLss] in next st for first fin, [1dc, dc2tog] twice, 1dc, [1FLss, 2ch, 1FLhtr, 2ch, 1FLss] in next st for second fin, 1dc, dc2tog, 1dc, ss in BL under tail fin to join (11 dc, 1 tail, 2 fins).

Change to Bridal White.

Round 8: 1BLdc in every st, ss to join (14 sts).

Stuff work.

Round 9: [Dc2tog] 7 times (7 sts).

Fasten off, add extra stuffing if needed and sew in ends. Attach eye beads on round 7, 5 sts apart, near the front fins.

WHALE SHARK

Materials

- 1.25mm-1.5mm (9/4 to 8/7/2 steel) crochet hook (1.5mm hook will produce slightly larger item)
- Scheepjes Sweet Treat in Dark Teal 401, Bridal White 105
- Embroidery needle
- 2mm black eye beads and cotton thread for sewing

Finished Size

15mm x 20mm x 45mm (19/32in x 25/32in x 149/64in)

Top of Body

The body is worked in 2 halves then sewn together.

Using Dark Teal, make 5PCIC (see Crochet Techniques).

Row 1 (head end): 1ch (does not count as a st throughout), turn, 2dc in first st, 3dc, 2dc in last st (7 sts).

Rows 2 to 4: 1ch, turn, 1dc in every st.

Row 5: 1ch, turn, dc2tog, 3dc, dc2tog (5 sts).

Row 6: 1ch, turn, 1dc in every st.

Row 7: 1ch, turn, dc2tog, 1dc, dc2tog (3 sts).

Row 8: 1ch, turn, 1dc in every st.

Row 9: 1ch, turn, dc2tog, 1dc (2 sts).

Row 10: 1ch, turn, dc2tog (1 st).

Row 11: 1ch, turn, 1dc (tail st)

Edging and Fins

1ch, 6dc up right side of body, [2ch, 1htr, 2ch, ss] in last dc just made for first fin, 5dc up right side of body, 5dc across 5PCIC sts, 6dc down other side of body, [2ch, 1htr, 2ch, ss] in last dc just made for second fin, 5dc down side towards tail, 1dc in row 11 st, ss to beg st of round.

Fasten off.

Top Fin

Using Dark Teal make a magic ring, [2ch, 2htr] into ring, fasten off. The magic ring makes the tip of the fin, sew upside down onto body between the fins. Using Bridal White, embroider little dashes on the head side of the body.

Underside of Body

Using Bridal White, make 5PCIC (see Crochet Techniques).

Rows 1 to 11: Rep rows 1 to 11 from top half of body.

Edging

1ch, 11dc up right side of body, 5dc across 5PCIC, 11dc down other side of body, 1dc in row 11 st, ss to beg st of round. Fasten off.

Join the two halves, sew the BLs together all around using whipstitch. Add stuffing. Attach eye beads on the seam line, 7 sts apart.

Tail

Round 1 (RS): Using Dark Teal, make a magic ring, 6dc into ring, ss to join (6 sts).

Round 2: 1ch (does not count as a st), 2dc in every st, ss to join (12 sts).

Fold in half, WS together, crochet together through the BLs to join, 1ch, 1htr, 3dc, [1dc, 3ch, 1dc in second and third ch from hook, 1dc] all in next st, 1dc.

Fasten off, sew in ends and use those ends to sew to the tail of the shark. Fin should be positioned vertically.

KILLER WHALE

Materials

- 1.25mm-1.5mm (9/4 to 8/7/2 steel) crochet hook (1.5mm hook will produce slightly larger item)
- Scheepjes Sweet Treat in Jet Back 110, Bridal White 105
- Embroidery needle
- 2mm black eye beads and cotton thread for sewing

Finished Size

20mm x 25mm x 50mm (²⁵⁄₃₂in x ⁶³⁄₆₄in x 1³¹⁄₃₂in)

Top of Body

Round 1: Using Jet Black make a magic ring, 5dc into ring, tighten ring but do not join round (5 sts, semi-circle shape).

Row 2: 1ch (does not count as a st throughout), turn, 5dc (5 sts).

Row 3: 1ch, turn, 2dc in first st, 3dc, 2dc in last st (7 sts).

Row 4: 1ch, turn, 2dc, 2dc in next st, 1dc, 2dc in next st, 2dc (9 sts).

Row 5: 1ch, turn, 2dc, 2dc in next st, 3dc, 2dc in next st, 2dc (11 sts).

Row 6: 1ch, turn, 1dc in every st.

Row 7: 1ch, turn, 2dc, dc2tog, 3dc, dc2tog, 2dc (9 sts).

Row 8: 1ch, turn, 2dc, dc2tog, 1dc, dc2tog, 2dc (7 sts).

Row 9: 1ch, turn, 1dc, dc2tog, 1dc, dc2tog, 1dc (5 sts).

Row 10: 1ch, turn, 1dc in every st.

Row 11: 1ch, turn, dc2tog, 1dc, dc2tog (3 sts).

Rows 12 to 13: 1ch, turn, 3dc (3 sts).

Row 14: 1ch, turn, 1dc, dc2tog (2 sts).

Row 15: 1ch, turn, 2dc (tail sts).

Edging and Fins

1ch, 1dc in the side of the last dc of row 15, 7dc up right side of whale, [3ch, 1tr, 3ch, ss] in FL of last dc just made, 6dc up same side towards head, 1dc in magic ring of round 1, 7dc down other side of whale, [3ch, 1tr, 3ch, ss] in FL of last dc just made for second fin, 7dc down same side towards tail end, 1dc in the 2 sts from row 15, ss in first st of round.

Change to Bridal White.

Round 1: Join with ss in BL underneath right fin, 13dc around the head to left side fin, 1BLdc behind left side fin, 18BLdc around tail end of whale back towards right fin, 1BLdc underneath right fin (33 sts).

Round 2: [Dc2tog, 1dc] 4 times around whale head, 9dc down left side of whale, [dc2tog] twice, 8dc up the right side, finishing under fin.

Round 3: [Dc2tog] 5 times, do not crochet rem sts in round.

Fasten off, stuff work, then use tail end to whipstitch the sides of the opening closed in the BLs.

Top Fin

Using Jet Black make a magic ring, [3ch, 2tr] in magic ring, fasten off. Makes triangle shape, magic ring corner is the tip of the fin. Use tail ends to sew to top of whale.

Using Bridal White, embroider patches behind the fin and on the side of the body, just in front of the fins. Attach eye beads to the front of the Bridal White patches, nearest to the tail.

Tail Fin (make 2)

Round 1 (RS): Using Jet Black make a magic ring, 6dc into ring, ss to join (6 sts).

Round 2: 1ch (does not count as a st), 2dc in every st, ss to join (12 sts).

Fold in half WS together to make a semi-circle, 2ch, join using 6BLss down side. No need for stuffing. Fasten off, leave ends for sewing. Sew both fins together at the corners, ss edges facing each other, then sew to the tail end.

Myth & Legend

Because who in the world wouldn't want their own tiny dragon!?

This chapter is utter whimsy and fantasy. Each character can be customised endlessly, to create a whole universe of creatures. Have a go at using metallic embroidery threads for a little extra magic, and add pipe cleaners to your stuffing to make your amis movable and posable. You can even combine the characters in this chapter with the designs in the Fairy Woodland chapter, so that they have their own little sidekicks.

The characters in this chapter have been made with Scheepjes Sweet Treat cotton threads and a 1.25mm (9/4 steel) hook, but they lend themselves really well to scaling up using DK yarn for playable dolls.

MERMAID & MERMAN

Materials

- 1.25mm-1.5mm (9/4 to 8/7/2 steel) crochet hook (1.5mm hook will produce slightly larger item)
- Scheepjes Sweet Treat in Candle Light 101, Sage Green 212, Colonial Rose 398, Ruby 517, Bluebird 247 for Mermaid; Moon Rock 254, Sage Green 212, Deep Ocean Green 391, Ruby 517 for Merman
- Embroidery needle
- 2mm black eye beads and cotton thread for sewing

Finished Size

40mm x 15mm x 15mm (1³⁷⁄₆₄in x ¹⁹⁄₃₂in x ¹⁹⁄₃₂in)

Head

Work in continuous rounds, starting with a magic ring in Candle Light/Moon Rock.

Round 1: 6dc into ring (6 sts).

Round 2: 2dc in every st (12 sts).

Round 3: [2dc in next st, 3dc] 3 times (15 sts).

Round 4: [2dc in next st, 4dc] 3 times (18 sts).

Round 5: [Dc2tog, 4dc] 3 times (15 sts).

Round 6: [Dc2tog, 3dc] 3 times (12 sts). Stuff work.

Round 7: [Dc2tog] 6 times (6 sts).

Fasten off and sew opening closed. Leave long end for sewing head onto the body.

Body

Round 1: Using Candle Light/Moon Rock, make a magic ring, 10dc into ring, ss to join (10 sts).

Round 2: 1ch (does not count as a st), 5dc, 2dc next st, 4dc, 1dc in same place as first st of this round (makes increase), ss to join (12 sts).

Round 3: 1dc in every st.

Change to Ruby/Deep Ocean Green.

Round 4: 1BLss in every st, invisible ss (see Crochet Techniques) to join.

Trim and sew in ends before changing to Colonial Rose/Sage Green.

Round 5: 1BLss in each st from round 3, behind the ss in round 4 (12 sts).

Rounds 6 and 7: 1dc in every st.

Round 8: [Dc2tog, 2dc] 3 times (9 sts). Stuff work.

Round 9: [Dc2tog, 1dc] 3 times (6 sts).

Tail Fins

Flatten opening and line up sts into pairs, with loop on hook in one corner. Crochet both sides together to join opening and add fin.

3ch, [2tr, 2ch, ss in second tr, 1tr] in first st, 3ch, ss in second st, 3ch, [2tr, 2ch, ss in second tr, tr, 3ch, ss] in third st. Fasten off and sew in ends.

Bikini Top (mermaid only)

Using Sage Green, make a magic ring, [2ch, tr2tog, 2ch, tr2tog] into ring, fasten off. Use tail ends to wrap around the torso and sew into place.

Arm (make 2)

Using Candle Light/Moon Rock, make 5PCIC, (see Crochet Techniques), fasten off and sew onto the sides of the torso. Sew the hands into place around the hip area or leave them loose.

Mermaid Hair

Using Bluebird, starting at the back of the head, make long repeated running stitches between the nape of the neck and the crown. Once there is enough coverage, bring the stitches forward gradually towards the front of the head then back to the nape. Thread the needle through a stitch of the head to make the hair parting. Repeat this process until the sides of the head are covered. Sew some long strands to the nape of the neck, for the hair braid. Thread 6 long strands across the front of the top of the head at the side parting. Make a plait down both sides of the face to the nape. Join with the strands at the nape to make one big braid down the back. Use one of the strands to wrap and knot the end of the braid. Trim excess strands.

Merman Hair

Round 1: Using Ruby, make a magic ring, 1ch, 6dc into ring, ss to join (6 sts).

Round 2: 3ch (counts as tr), 1puff in same st, [1tr, 1puff] in each rem st, ss in beg 3-ch to join (6 puffs, 6 tr).

Round 3: [3ch, 2trCL in tr at base of 3ch, ss in next tr] 6 times.

Fasten off and sew hair onto head.

For more on adding hair, see the techniques section

Finishing for Both

Attach eye beads 4 sts apart. Using Candle Light/Moon Rock sew 3 small dashes between the eyes to make a nose. Sew head onto body.

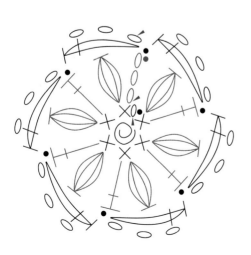

Merman Hair

FAIRY

Materials

- 1.25mm-1.5mm (9/4 to 8/7/2 steel) crochet hook (1.5mm hook will produce slightly larger item)
- Scheepjes Sweet Treat in Candle Light 101, Bluebird 247, Rust 388, Cherry 413
- DMC Light Effects in Gemstones E130 (optional)
- Embroidery needle
- 2mm black eye beads and cotton thread for sewing

Finished Size

50mm x 25mm x 20mm (1³¹⁄₃₂in x ⁶³⁄₆₄in x ²⁵⁄₃₂in)

Head

Work in continuous rounds, starting with a magic ring in Candle Light.

Round 1: 6dc into ring (6 sts).

Round 2: 2dc in every st (12 sts).

Round 3: [2dc in next st, 3dc] 3 times (15 sts).

Round 4: [2dc in next st, 4dc] 3 times (18 sts).

Round 5: [Dc2tog, 4dc] 3 times (15 sts).

Round 6: [Dc2tog, 3dc] 3 times (12 sts). Stuff work.

Round 7: [Dc2tog] 6 times (6 sts).

Fasten off and sew opening closed. Leave long end for sewing head onto the body.

Hair

Using Rust, work rounds 1 to 3 as for merman hair.

Bun

Using Rust, make a magic ring, 3ch, 4trbobble (see Crochet Techniques), 3ch, 4trbobble in first bobble, fasten off and fold in the middle. Use thread ends to sew the sides together if needed, then sew onto the hair. Sew the hair onto the head, positioned tilted backwards slightly so that the bun is not directly on top of the head. Attach eye beads 4 sts apart. Use tail end of the head to sew 3 small dashes between the eyes to make a nose.

Body

Round 1: Using Bluebird, make a magic ring, 10dc into ring, ss to join (10 sts).

Round 2: 1ch (does not count as a st), 5dc, 2dc next st, 4dc, 1dc in same place as first st of this round (makes increase), ss to join (12 sts).

Rounds 3 to 4: 1dc in every st.

Round 5: [2FLdc in next st, 2FLdc] 4 times (16 sts).

Pause at round 5, do not fasten off.

Legs

Round 1: Using Candle Light, starting in the first BL of round 4, 1BLdc in every st.

Round 2: 3dc, skip 6 sts, 3dc (6 sts).

Rounds 3 to 8: Working in continuous rounds, 1dc in every st (6 sts).

Fasten off and sew in ends, no need to stuff the legs. Stuff body before starting second leg. Repeat round 3 a further 7 times into rem 6 sts of round 2 for second leg.

Dress

Continue from round 5 of body in Bluebird.

Rounds 6 and 7: Work in continuous rounds. 1dc in every st (16 sts).

Round 8: [ss in next st, 2htr in next st] 8 times. Fasten off and sew in ends.

Sleeve and Arm (make 2)

Using Bluebird, make a magic ring, [3ch, 6tr] into ring, ss in 3ch sp, fasten off, leaving long ends.

Using Candle Light make 6PCIC (see Crochet Techniques), fasten off.

Insert the arms into the sleeves and use the ends to sew onto the body.

Fairy Wings

Round 1: Using Cherry, make a magic ring, into the ring work [4ch, 3dtr, 4ch, ss] for first large wing, 2ch, 1htr, 2ch, ss, [4ch, 3dtr, 4ch, ss] for second large wing.

Round 2: 1ch, turn, 4dc in 4ch sp, [1dc, 2ch, 1dc] in first dtr, 1dc in next 2 dtr, [2dc, 2ch, ss] in 4ch sp, [(ss, 2ch, 2tr, 2ch, ss) in next 2ch sp] twice for bottom wings, [ss, 2ch, 2dc] in 4ch sp of large wing, 1dc in next 2 dtr, [1dc, 2ch, 1dc] in last dtr, 4dc in 4ch sp, 1ch, ss in magic ring.

Fasten off and sew in ends.

Round 3 (optional): Turn work, surface crochet ss into each st and ch, using one strand of Gemstones Light Effects thread.

Finishing

Sew head onto body using the thread end from the head. Wrap the neck area once with Bluebird to make a collar and cover any stitching. Make a running stitch in Cherry across the waist of the body. Sew the wings to the back of the body.

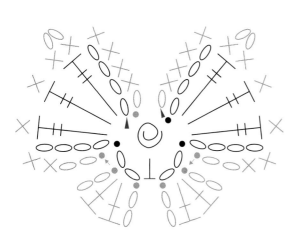

Fairy Wings

WITCH

Materials

- 1.25mm-1.5mm (9/4 to 8/7/2 steel) crochet hook (1.5mm hook will produce slightly larger item)
- Scheepjes Sweet Treat in Jet Black 110, Amethyst 240, Sage Green 212, Tyrian Purple 128, Topaz 179
- Gütermann hand quilting cotton in Black 5201
- Embroidery needle
- 2mm black eye beads and cotton thread for sewing

Finished Size

60mm x 25mm x 25mm (2²³⁄₆₄in x 6³⁄₆₄in x 6³⁄₆₄in)

Head

Work in continuous rounds, starting with a magic ring in Sage Green.

Round 1: 6dc in ring (6 sts).

Round 2: 2dc in every st (12 sts).

Round 3: [2dc in next st, 3dc] 3 times (15 sts).

Round 4: [2dc in next st, 4dc] 3 times (18 sts).

Round 5: [Dc2tog, 4dc] 3 times (15 sts).

Round 6: [Dc2tog, 3dc] 3 times (12 sts).

Stuff work.

Round 7: [Dc2tog] 6 times (6 sts).

Fasten off and sew opening closed. Leave long end for sewing head to body.

Body

Round 1: Using Amethyst, make a magic ring, 10dc into ring, ss to join (10 sts).

Round 2: 1ch (does not count as a st), 5dc, 2dc next st, 4dc, 1dc in same place as first st of this round (makes increase), ss to join (12 sts).

Rounds 3 and 4: 1dc in every st.

Round 5: [2FLdc in next st, 2FLdc] 4 times (16 sts).

Pause at round 5, do not fasten off.

Legs

Round 1: Using Sage Green, starting in the first BL of Round 4, 1BLdc in every st.

Round 2: 3dc, skip 6 sts, 3dc (6 sts).

Rounds 3 to 7: Working in continuous rounds, 1dc in every st (6 sts).

Change to Jet Black for the shoe.

Round 8: 1dc in every st.

Fasten off, no need to stuff the legs. Stuff body before starting second leg. Repeat round 3 a further 6 times into rem 6 sts of round 2 for second leg. Use Jet Black thread ends to add extra thickness around the edges of the shoes. Embroider French knots in Topaz for shoe buckles.

Dress

Continue from round 5 of body in Amethyst.

Rounds 6 to 7: 1dc in every st (16 sts).

Round 8: [2dc in next st, 3dc] 4 times (20 sts).

Rounds 9 to 12: 1dc in every st.

Fasten off and make an invisible ss to join to the first st (see Crochet Techniques).

Arm (make 2)

Using Sage Green, make a magic ring, 3ch, tr2tog in magic ring, fold over and ss in magic ring, make 4PCIC (see Crochet Techniques). Fasten off.

Sleeve (make 2)

Round 1: Using Amethyst, make a magic ring, 3ch, [tr2tog] 6 times into ring, ss to join (6 sts).

Round 2: 1ch, 1BLdc in every st, ss to join.

Round 3: Work in continuous rounds from this point onward, 6dc.

Round 4: [2dc in next st, 2dc] twice (8 sts).

Ss into next st before fastening off.

Insert the PCIC section of the arm into the sleeve so that only the hand sticks out, and sew sleeves onto the sides of the body.

Hat

Work in continuous rounds, starting with a magic ring in Tyrian Purple.

Round 1: 6dc into ring (6 sts).

Round 2: 6dc.

Round 3: [2dc in next st, 1dc] 3 times (9 sts).

Round 4: [2dc in next st, 2dc] 3 times (12 sts).

Round 5: [2dc in next st, 3dc] 3 times (15 sts).

Round 6: 1dc in every st.

Round 7: [2dc in next st, 4dc] 3 times (18 sts).

Round 8: 1dc in every st.

Round 9: [1FLdc, 2FLdc in next st] 9 times (27 sts).

Round 10: 1back-dc (crab st) in every st.

Fasten off and sew in ends. Use Jet Black to work surface crochet onto round 9.

Finishing

Using Tyrian Purple, embroider a little square onto the skirt of the dress then add Black sts with the Gütermann hand quilting cotton to make a patch. Use Jet Black to add a belt using running stitches across the waist, then a little square in Topaz for the buckle.

Pigtails

Sew head onto the body before adding the hair. Use Black thread to sew a running stitch from the front of the hairline to the nape of the neck, then back to the front hairline, to act as an anchor point for attaching hair. Thread long lengths of Black thread onto the running stitch, wrapping around a credit card at the same time to keep the threads consistent in length. Once completed, trim threads to desired length, wrap Black thread around the lengths to make the pigtails. Sew hat to the top of the head, tilted back slightly. Attach eye beads to face.

WIZARD

Materials

- 1.25mm-1.5mm (9/4 to 8/7/2 steel) crochet hook (1.5mm hook will produce slightly larger item)
- Scheepjes Sweet Treat in Topaz 179, Black Coffee 162, Candle Light 101, Moon Rock 254, Ruby 517
- Embroidery needle
- 2mm black eye beads and cotton thread for sewing

Finished Size

60mm x 25mm x 25mm (2²³⁄₆₄in x 6³⁄₆₄in x 6³⁄₆₄in)

Head

Using Topaz, work as for witch's head.

Hat

Using Black Coffee, work as for witch's hat. Use Ruby for surface crochet on round 9.

Body

Round 1: Using Moon Rock, make a magic ring, 10dc into ring, ss to join (10 sts).

Round 2: 1ch (does not count as a st), 5dc, 2dc next st, 4dc, 1dc in same place as first st of this round (makes increase), ss to join (12 sts).

Round 3: 1dc in every st.

Round 4: [2FLdc in next st, 2FLdc] 4 times (16 sts).

Pause at round 4, do not fasten off.

Legs

Round 1: Using Topaz, starting in the first BL of round 3, 1BLdc in every st.

Round 2: 3dc, skip 6 sts, 3dc (6 sts).

Rounds 3 to 8: Working in continuous rounds, 1dc in every st (6 sts).

Fasten off and sew in ends, no need to stuff the legs. Stuff body before starting second leg. Repeat round 3 a further 7 times into rem 6 sts of round 2 for second leg.

Dress

Continue from round 4 of body in Moon Rock.

Rounds 5 and 6: 1dc in every st (16 sts).

Round 7: [2dc in next st, 3dc] 4 times (20 sts).

Rounds 8 to 13: 1dc in every st.

Fasten off.

Arm (make 2)

Using Topaz, make a magic ring, 3ch, tr2tog in magic ring, fold over and ss in magic ring, make 4PCIC (see Crochet Techniques). Fasten off.

Sleeve (make 2)

Work in continuous rounds, make a magic ring in Moon Rock.

Round 1: 5dc into ring (5 sts).

Round 2: 1dc in every st.

Round 3: 2dc, [1htr, 1tr, 1htr] in next st, 2dc (7 sts).

Round 4: 3dc, [1htr, 1tr, 1htr] in round 3 centre tr, 3dc (9 sts).

Round 5: 5dc to tip of sleeve, fasten off, do not crochet rest of round.

Insert the PCIC section of the arm into the sleeve so that only the hand sticks out and sew sleeves onto the sides of the body.

Beard

Special stitches: bobble – 4 treble st bobble (see Crochet Techniques)

Using Candle Light, make a magic ring, [4ch, 1bobble, 3ch, ss] into magic ring, pull to close. Use thread ends to sew onto face.

Hair

Sew head onto the body first for easier handling. Using Candle Light, make 2 rows of stitches from the front hairline to just after the crown of the head. Wrap hair onto those stitches as for witch's pigtails. Trim to desired length, make into a low ponytail, tying into place with Ruby thread. Sew hat onto head, tilting backwards slightly. Sew eye beads onto the head at either side of the beard.

Waist Tie

Wrap 2 lengths of Black Coffee thread around the waist and sew them to secure with one stitch at the tummy. Knot the 2 lengths together and trim, keeping them long. Cover the tummy stitch with a couple of stitches in Ruby.

UNICORN

Materials

- 1.25mm-1.5mm (9/4 to 8/7/2 steel) crochet hook (1.5mm hook will produce slightly larger item)
- Scheepjes Sweet Treat in Candle Light 101, Colonial Rose 398, Bluebird 247, Ruby 517
- Embroidery needle
- 2mm black eye beads and cotton thread for sewing

Finished Size

40mm x 15mm x 40mm (1³⁷⁄₆₄in x 1⁹⁄₃₂in x 1³⁷⁄₆₄in)

Chest

Work in continuous rounds, starting with a magic ring in Candle Light.

Round 1: 6dc into ring (6 sts).

Round 2: 2dc in every st (12 sts).

Round 3: [2dc in next st, 1dc] 6 times (18 sts).

Round 4: [2dc in next st, 2dc] 6 times (24 sts).

Place a marker in the fifth st from each end of the last round.

Neck

Round 5: Work 5dc (up to and including first marked st), fold circle RS facing outwards, 1dc into second marked st, 4dc (10 sts).

Round 6: 3dc, [dc2tog] twice, 3dc (8 sts).

Round 7: 2dc, [dc2tog] twice, 2dc (6 sts).

Fasten off, leave a long length for sewing, do not sew opening closed.

Main Body

Round 8: Using Candle Light join with ss in second marked st from round 4, 1dc in same st, 1dc in next 14 sts, 1dc in first marked st from round 4 (16 sts).

Rounds 9 to 11: Working in continuous rounds, 1dc in every st. Stuff work.

Round 12: [Dc2tog] 8 times (8 sts).

Fasten off, add more stuffing and sew in ends.

Head

Work in continuous rounds, starting with a magic ring in Candle Light.

Round 1: 6dc into ring (6 sts).

Round 2: [2dc in next st, 1dc] 3 times (9 sts).

Round 3: 1dc in every st.

Round 4: [2dc in next st, 2dc] 3 times (12 sts).

Round 5: 1dc in every st.

Round 6: [1FLss, 2ch, 1FLtr, 2ch, ss in tr, 2ch, 1FLss] in first st to make ear, 3dc, [1FLss, 2ch, 1FLtr, 2ch, ss in tr, 2ch, 1FLss] in next st to make second ear, 7dc.

Stuff work.

Round 7: [Dc2tog] 6 times (6 sts).

Fasten off and sew opening closed and sew in ends. Use yarn end from the neck to sew head and body together.

Leg (make 4)

Round 1: Using Colonial Rose, make a magic ring, 6dc into ring, ss to join (6 sts).

Round 2: 1ch (does not count as a st), 1dc in every st, ss to join.

Fasten off, change to Candle Light.

Rounds 3 to 6: Work in continuous rounds, 1dc in every st.

Ss in next st, fasten off, leaving a long end for sewing. Use excess threads from rounds 1 and 3 as stuffing. Sew 2 of the legs at the front under the neck opening. The magic ring from round 1 of body should be between the legs. Sew the other 2 legs at the back at rounds 10 to 11.

Mane

Special stitches: bobble – 5 treble st bobble (see Crochet Techniques)

Make 1 bobble in each of Ruby, Bluebird and Colonial Rose. Make a magic ring, [3ch, 1bobble] into ring, fasten off. Use the thread ends to sew between the ears at the top of the head and down the back of the neck.

Horn

Using Colonial Rose, make 3PCIC (see Crochet Techniques). Fasten off and use thread ends to sew onto the head in front of the first bobble stitch.

Tail

Using Ruby, Colonial Rose and Bluebird, sew long lengths of thread to the back end of the body, just above the sewn-in areas of the last round. Use a thread of your choice to wrap around the base of the tail to disguise any sewing. Trim tail to desired lengths.

Eyes

Sew bead eyes to round 4 of the head, 4 sts apart, just in front of the base of the ears.

CERBERUS

Materials

- 1.25mm-1.5mm (9/4 to 8/7/2 steel) crochet hook (1.5mm hook will produce slightly larger item)
- Scheepjes Sweet Treat in Jet Black 110, Rust 388, Bluebird 247, Cherry 413, Black Coffee 162
- Embroidery needle
- 2mm black eye beads and cotton thread for sewing

Finished Size

25mm x 45mm x 45mm (6³⁄₆₄in x 1⁴⁹⁄₆₄in x 1⁴⁹⁄₆₄in)

Head (make 3)

Work in continuous rounds, starting with a magic ring in Rust.

Round 1: 6dc into ring (6 sts).

Round 2: [2dc in next st, 1dc] 3 times (9 sts).

Round 3: 1dc in every st.

Round 4: 3dc in each of next 3 sts, 6dc (15 sts).

Round 5: 1dc in every st.

Round 6: 2dc, [1FLss, 1ch, 1FLhtr, 2ch, 1FLhtr, 1ch, 1FLss] in next st to make ear, 3dc, [1FLss, 1ch, 1FLhtr, 2ch, 1FLhtr, 1ch, 1FLss] in next st to make second ear, 2dc, [dc2tog] 3 times (12 sts).

Round 7: 2dc, 1BLdc, dc3tog, 1BLdc, 5dc (10 sts).

Rounds 8 and 9: 1dc in every st.

Fasten off, leave long length for sewing. Stuff but do not sew opening closed

Body

Work in continuous rounds, starting with a magic ring in Rust.

Round 1: 6dc into ring (6 sts).

Round 2: 2dc in every st (12 sts).

Round 3: [2dc in next st, 1dc] 6 times (18 sts).

Rounds 4 to 10: 1dc in every st.

Round 11: [Dc2tog, 1dc] 6 times (12 sts).

Round 12: 1dc in every st.

Stuff work.

Round 13: [Dc2tog] 6 times (6 sts).

Fasten off and sew in ends.

Leg (make 4)

Work in continuous rounds, starting with a magic ring in Rust.

Round 1: 6dc into ring (6 sts).

Round 2: [2dc in next st, 1dc] 3 times (9 sts).

Rounds 3 and 4: 1dc in every st.

Fasten off and stuff. Do not sew opening closed.

Tail

Special stitches: bobble – 5 treble st bobble (see Crochet Techniques)

Make a magic ring, [3ch, 1bobble] into ring, fasten off. Use the thread ends to sew the tail to the back end of the body, slightly above the magic ring from round 1.

Assembly

Sew 1 head to the narrow end of the body, like a regular dog. Sew the other 2 on either side to make a row of heads. Sew the legs to the underside of the body with the front 2 legs close to where the heads are.

Collar

Make 1 in each of Bluebird, Cherry and Jet Black; work 11ch, fasten off, wrap around the neck and use thread ends to sew into place.

Tongue (make 3)

Using Cherry, make 3ch, fasten off, fold in half and use thread ends to sew to the face.

Nose

Using Black Coffee, embroider stitches from the magic ring of the head to the stitch above to make the nose shape.

Eyes

Sew eye beads on round 4 where the increases form the brow.

DRAGON

Materials

- 1.25mm-1.5mm (9/4 to 8/7/2 steel) crochet hook (1.5mm hook will produce slightly larger item)
- Scheepjes Sweet Treat in Topaz 179, Candle Light 101, Ruby 517
- Embroidery needle
- 2mm black eye beads and cotton thread for sewing
- Pipe cleaner or jewellery wire

Finished Size

35mm x 25mm x 70mm (1⅜in x 6¾₄in x 2¾in) (with outstretched tail)

Chest

Work in continuous rounds, starting with a magic ring in Topaz.

Round 1: 6dc into ring (6 sts).

Round 2: 2dc in every st (12 sts).

Round 3: [2dc in next st, 1dc] 6 times (18 sts).

Round 4: [2dc in next st, 2dc] 6 times (24 sts).

Place a marker in the fourth st from each end of the last round.

Neck

Round 5: Work 4dc (up to and including first marked st), fold circle RS facing outwards, 1dc into second marked st, 3dc (8 sts).

Rounds 6 to 8: 1dc in every st.

Head

Round 9: [2dc in next st] 3 times to make jaw, 2dc, 2dc in next st for top of head, 2dc (12 sts).

Rounds 10 to 12: 1dc in every st.

Round 13: 6dc, [dc2tog] 3 times (9 sts).

Round 14: Dc2tog, 5dc, dc2tog (7 sts).

Fasten off and sew opening closed. Fold tip of pipe cleaner twice to make rough shape of the head. Insert into the head and neck, leaving the rest sticking out for the body and tail.

Main Body

Round 15: Using Topaz join with ss in second marked st from Round 4, 1dc in same st, 1dc in next 16 sts, 1dc in first marked st from round 4 (18 sts).

Rounds 16 to 20: 1dc in every st.

Round 21: 2dc, dc2tog, 12dc, dc2tog (16 sts).

Round 22: 2dc, dc2tog, 10dc, dc2tog (14 sts).

Round 23: 2dc, dc2tog, 8dc, dc2tog (12 sts).

Add stuffing to the body around the pipe cleaner.

Tail

Round 24: 1dc in every st (12 sts).

Round 25: 2dc, dc2tog, 6dc, dc2tog (10 sts).

Round 26: 1dc in every st.

Round 27: 2dc, dc2tog, 4dc, dc2tog (8 sts).

Rounds 28 to 32: 1dc in every st.

Trim the pipe cleaner fibres with scissors if needed as the tail gets narrower.

Round 33: Dc2tog, 6dc (7 sts).

Round 34: 1dc in every st.

Round 35: Dc2tog, 5dc (6 sts).

Round 36: 1dc in every st.

Trim pipe cleaner, fasten off and sew opening closed.

Front Leg (make 2)

Work in continuous rounds, starting with a magic ring in Topaz.

Round 1: 6dc into ring (6 sts).

Rounds 2 to 6: 1dc in every st.

Fasten off, use thread end from magic ring to stuff the legs. Sew to the chest area on rounds 2 to 3. The magic ring of round 1 should be in the middle and slightly above the legs.

Back Leg (make 2)

Work in continuous rounds, starting with a magic ring in Topaz.

Round 1: 6dc into ring (6 sts).

Round 2: 1dc in every st.

Round 3: 3tr in each of next 2 sts, 4dc (10 sts).

Round 4: 7dc, do not crochet rest of round.

Fasten off, use thread end from magic ring to stuff the legs. Sew in a seated position with the leg opening attached to rounds 22 to 23 of main body.

Left Wing

Round 1: Using Topaz, make a magic ring, [4ch, 3dtr, 4ch, ss] into magic ring.

Round 2: Do not turn work, 1ch, 1dc in magic ring, 2ch, [ss, 2ch, ss] in 4ch sp, [ss, 2ch, ss] in next 2 dtr, [ss, 2ch, 2htr] in next dtr, 4dc in 4ch sp, 1dc in magic ring, [2ch, ss] in first dc. Fasten off.

Right Wing

Round 1: Using Topaz, make a magic ring, [4ch, 3dtr, 4ch, ss] into magic ring.

Round 2: Do not turn work, 1ch, 1dc in magic ring, 4dc in 4ch sp, [2htr, 2ch, ss] in dtr, [ss, 2ch, ss] in next 2 dtr, [ss, 2ch, ss] in 4ch sp, 2ch, 1dc in magic ring, 2ch, ss in first dc. Fasten off.

Sew wings to the side of the dragon, RS facing outwards.

Ear (make 2)

Using Topaz, make a magic ring, 4ch, 1dc in third ch from hook, 1dc in next ch, ss in magic ring. Fasten off and use ends to sew to side of head.

Horn (make 2)

Using Candle Light make 2PCIC (see Crochet Techniques), use ends to sew to the top of the head.

Tail Spike

Using Ruby, make a magic ring, [2ch, 2tr, 2ch, ss in second tr, 1tr, 3ch, ss] in magic ring. Fasten off, leaving a long tail to make spine.

Left Wing

Right Wing

Spine

Use the tail end from the tail spike to make a running stitch along the top of the tail, back, neck and top of head, finishing between the ears. Whipstitch back over the stitches just made, to give a textured effect that covers any gaps in the stitching.

Face Details

Using Topaz, add 2 French knots for nostrils. Sew eye beads to the side of the head just in front of the base of the ears.

SEA SERPENT

Materials

- 1.25mm-1.5mm (9/4 to 8/7/2 steel) crochet hook (1.5mm hook will produce slightly larger item)
- Scheepjes Sweet Treat in Deep Ocean Green 391, Dark Teal 401
- Embroidery needle
- 2mm black eye beads and cotton thread for sewing
- Pipe cleaners or jewellery wire

Finished Size

35mm x 8mm x 80mm (1⅜in x ⁵⁄₁₆in x 3⁵⁄₃₂in) (with outstretched tail)

Head

Work in continuous rounds, starting with a magic ring in Deep Ocean Green.

Round 1: 6dc into ring (6 sts).

Round 2: [2dc in next st, 1dc] 3 times (9 sts).

Round 3: 1dc in every st.

Round 4: [2dc in next st, 2dc] 3 times (12 sts).

Round 5: [2dc in next st, 3dc] 3 times (15 sts).

Round 6: [2dc in next st, 4dc] 3 times (18 sts).

Crown

Round 7: *[1FLss, 1ch, 1FLhtr, 2ch, 1FLhtr, 1ch, 1FLss] in next st, 1FLss in next 2 sts, rep from * once more, [1FLss, 1ch, 1FLhtr, 2ch, 1FLhtr, 1ch, 1FLss] in next st, [1dc, dc2tog, dc2tog] twice, 1dc (14 sts).

Round 8: 7BLdc, 1dc, [dc2tog, 1dc] twice (12 sts).

Round 9: [1dc, dc2tog] twice, 6dc (10 sts).

Neck

Rounds 10 to 21: 1dc in every st (10 sts).

Fold a pipe cleaner in half, fold the bent end at the tip once or twice to get the general shape of the head, insert into the neck and head. Add more stuffing as you go from this point onwards. Crochet around the rem pipe cleaner as you go.

Round 22: [2dc in next st, 4dc] twice (12 sts).

Rounds 23 to 25: 1dc in every st.

Main Body

Round 26: [2dc in next st, 5dc] twice (14 sts).

Rounds 27 to 32: 1dc in every st.

Round 33: [Dc2tog, 5dc] twice (12 sts).

Rounds 34 and 35: 1dc in every st.

Round 36: [Dc2tog, 4dc] twice (10 sts).

Rounds 37 to 39: 1dc in every st.

Round 40: [Dc2tog, 3dc] twice (8 sts).

Rounds 41 to 43: 1dc in every st.

Round 44: Dc2tog, 6dc (7 sts).

Rounds 45 and 46: 1dc in every st.

Round 47: Dc2tog, 5dc (6 sts).

Rounds 48 and 49: 1dc in every st.

Round 50: Dc2tog, 4dc (5 sts).

Round 51: 1dc in every st.

Fasten off, trim pipe cleaner to size and sew in ends.

Neck Fin (make 2)

Using Dark Teal, make a magic ring, 4ch, ss in third ch from hook, 1htr in magic ring, 2ch, ss in htr, 2ch, ss in second ch from hook, 2ch, ss in magic ring. Fasten off. Pull magic ring closed and use ends to sew onto the sides of the neck.

Spine

Using Dark Teal and leaving a long tail, work [3ch, ss in second ch from hook] 16 times. Fasten off. Position first repeat at top of head behind crown. Using the long tail sew the spine along the top of the body with the spikes evenly spaced.

Tail Spike

Using Dark Teal, make a magic ring, [2ch, 2tr, 2ch, ss in tr, 1tr, 2ch, ss] in magic ring. Fasten off. Pull closed and use tail ends to sew to the end of the tail.

Eyes

Sew eye beads to round 4 of head on side of face.

Neck Fin

Tail Spike

Spine

GNOME

Materials

- 1.25mm-1.5mm (9/4 to 8/7/2 steel) crochet hook (1.5mm hook will produce slightly larger item)
- Scheepjes Sweet Treat in Topaz 179, Deep Ocean Green 391, Rust 388, Bridal White 105, Hot Red 115, Ginger Gold 383, Moon Rock 254, Sage Green 212
- Embroidery needle

Finished Size

50mm x 30mm x 20mm (1³¹⁄₃₂in x 1³⁄₁₆in x ²⁵⁄₃₂in)

Head

Work in continuous rounds, starting with a magic ring in Topaz.

Round 1: 6dc into ring (6 sts).

Round 2: 2dc in every st (12 sts).

Round 3: [2dc in next st, 2dc] 4 times (16 sts).

Round 4: [2dc in next st, 3dc] 4 times (20 sts).

Round 5: [Dc2tog, 3dc] 4 times (16 sts).

Round 6: [Dc2tog, 2dc] 4 times (12 sts).

Round 7: [Dc2tog] 6 times (6 sts).

Hat and Hair

Work in continuous rounds, starting with a magic ring in Hot Red.

Round 1: 6dc into ring (6 sts).

Round 2: [2dc in next st, 1dc] 3 times (9 sts).

Round 3: [2dc in next st, 2dc] 3 times (12 sts).

Round 4: [2dc in next st, 3dc] 3 times (15 sts).

Round 5: [2dc in next st, 4dc] 3 times (18 sts).

Round 6: [2dc in next st, 5dc] 3 times (21 sts).

Round 7: 1dc in every st.

Round 8: 1FLdc in every st.

Change to Bridal White.

Round 9: 1BLdc in every st of round 7, ss to join (21 sts).

Round 10: *3ch, dtr3tog in st at base of 3ch, skip 2 sts, ss in next st, rep from * 6 more times, working last ss into first st of round (7 bobbles of hair under hat).

Fasten off, leaving a long tail end. Stuff hat and position on the head so that it is tilted back slightly. Use Bridal White tail end to sew hair onto the head at the slip stitches.

Beard

Using Bridal White, make a magic ring, [3ch, tr3tog] into magic ring, [3ch, tr3tog in bobble just made] twice.

Fasten off leaving long tail ends for sewing. Position on the bottom of the head so that the middle bobble covers the chin and the side bobbles join the hair. Sew into place using the tail ends.

Eyes

Sew eye beads in the space between the hair and beard about 4 sts apart.

Body

Round 1: Using Deep Ocean Green, make a magic ring, 6dc into ring, ss to join (6 sts).

Round 2: 1ch (does not count as a st throughout), 2dc in every st, ss to join (12 sts).

Round 3: 1ch, [2dc in next st, 3dc] 3 times, ss to join (15 sts).

Round 4: 1ch [2dc in next st, 2dc] 5 times, ss to join (20 sts).

Change to Rust.

Round 5: 1BLdc in every st, ss to join.

Round 6: 1ch, 1dc in every st, ss to join.

Legs

Work in continuous rounds, stuffing as you go.

Round 7: 5dc, skip 10 sts, 1dc in rem 5 sts (10 sts).

Round 8: 1dc in every st.

Round 9: [Dc2tog] 5 times (5 sts).

Fasten off, add extra stuffing, and sew in ends. Join Rust to first of 10 sts not yet worked from round 6.

Rounds 7 and 8: 1dc in every st.

Round 9: [Dc2tog] 5 times (5 sts).

Fasten off, add extra stuffing, and sew in ends.

Arm (make 2)

Using Topaz, make a magic ring, [3ch, tr2tog] in magic ring, fold over and ss into magic ring, make 4PCIC (see Crochet Techniques).

Round 1: Using Deep Ocean Green, make a magic ring, 3ch (counts as a tr), 5tr into ring, ss to join (6 sts).

Rounds 2 to 4: Working in continuous rounds, 1dc in every st (6 sts).

Ss into next st, fasten off. Insert the PCIC section of the arm into the sleeve so that only the hand sticks out, and sew onto the sides of the body.

Belt

Using Moon Rock and Ginger Gold, stitch a belt and buckle between the Deep Ocean Green and Rust stitches. Using Sage Green, add 3 buttons to the top half of the gnome.

GOBLIN

Materials

- 1.25mm-1.5mm (9/4 to 8/7/2 steel) crochet hook (1.5mm hook will produce slightly larger item)
- Scheepjes Sweet Treat in Sage Green 212, Moon Rock 254, Candle Light 101
- Embroidery needle
- 2mm black eye beads and cotton thread for sewing

Finished Size

32mm x 40mm x 15mm (1¹⁷⁄₆₄in x 1³⁷⁄₆₄in x 1⁹⁄₃₂in)

Head

Work in continuous rounds, starting with a magic ring in Sage Green.

Round 1: 6dc into ring (6 sts).

Round 2: 2dc in every st (12 sts).

Round 3: [2dc in next st, 2dc] 4 times (16 sts).

Round 4: [2dc in next st, 3dc] 4 times (20 sts).

Round 5: 1dc in every st.

Round 6: [Dc2tog, 3dc] 4 times (16 sts).

Round 7: [Dc2tog, 2dc] 4 times (12 sts). Stuff work.

Round 8: [Dc2tog] 6 times (6 sts). Fasten off and sew in ends.

Ear (make 2)

Using Sage Green make 4ch, 1dc in second ch from hook, 1htr in next ch, 3tr in next ch, 2ch, ss in last tr worked for tip of ear, 2tr in same ch as last tr, 1htr on other side of next ch, 1dc in next ch, ss to next ch. Fasten off, pinch the base of the ear to give it a fold and sew into place on the sides of the head, about halfway down.

Horn (make 2)

Using Candle Light, make 2PCIC (see Crochet Techniques) or 3ch, starting in first st or second ch from hook, 1dc in next 2 sts. Fasten off and use thread ends to sew onto top of head on round 2, between the ears.

Body

Round 1: Using Moon Rock make a magic ring, 10dc into ring, ss to join (10 sts).

Round 2: 1ch (does not count as a st throughout), 5dc, 2dc in next st, 4dc, 1dc in first st of round 1, ss to join (12 sts).

Round 3: 1ch, 1dc in every st, ss to join.

Round 4: 1ch, [2dc in next st, 2dc] 4 times, ss to join (16 sts).

Round 5: 1ch, 1FLdc in every st, ss to join.

Pause crocheting in Moon Rock, do not fasten off, change to Sage Green to start legs, work in continuous rounds.

Round 1: Ss to join, 1ch in first BL of round 4, 1BLdc in every st (16 sts).

Round 2: 4dc, skip 8 sts, 4dc (8 sts). Stuff as you go.

Round 3: 1dc in every st (8 sts).

Round 4: [Dc2tog] 4 times (4 sts).

Fasten off and sew opening closed. Join Sage Green to first of rem 8 sts from round 1.

Rounds 2 and 3: 1dc in every st (8 sts).

Stuff as you go.

Round 4: [Dc2tog] 4 times (4 sts).

Fasten off and sew opening closed.

Pick up Moon Rock from round 5, work in continuous rounds from this point onwards.

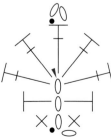

Ear

Sleeve

Round 6: [2dc in next st, 3dc] 4 times (20 sts).

Rounds 7 and 8: 1dc in every st.

Ss in the next st, fasten off.

Arm (make 2)

Using Sage Green, make a magic ring, [3ch, tr2tog] in magic ring, fold over and ss into magic ring, make 4PCIC (see Crochet Techniques).

Sleeve (make 2)

Work in continuous rounds, starting with a magic ring in Moon Rock.

Round 1: 5dc into ring (5 sts).

Round 2: 5dc.

Round 3: 2dc, [1htr, 1tr, 1htr] in next st, 2dc (7 sts).

Round 4: 3dc, [1htr, 1tr, 1htr] in next st, 3dc (9 sts).

Round 5: 5dc to tip of sleeve, fasten off and do not crochet rest of round.

Insert the PCIC section of the arm into the sleeve so that only the hand sticks out and sew onto the sides of the body. Sew head onto the top of body using Moon Rock.

Neck Wrap

Using Moon Rock, make 26ch, starting in second ch from hook, 1dc into the BL of each ch to make a strip (25 sts). This makes a better finished edge down the side. Fasten off long lengths for sewing. Wrap the strip around the neck and diagonally across the front of the body, making sure to overlap the end of the strip that is on the neck. Sew into place.

Eyes

Attach eye beads either side of face beneath the horns.

Techniques

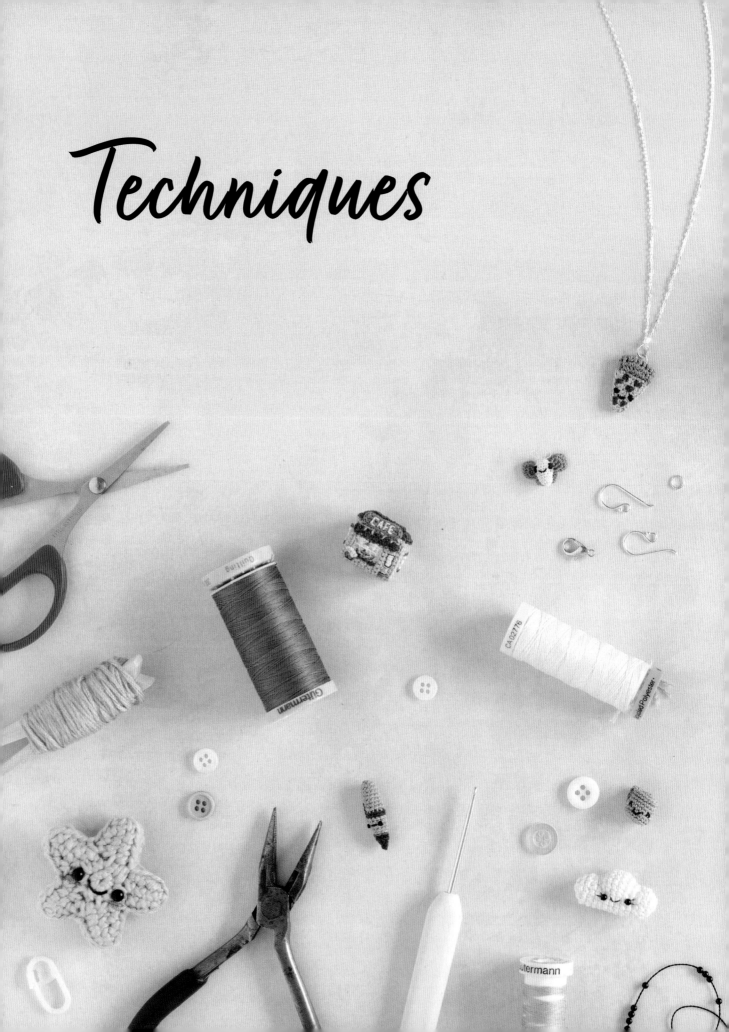

Crocheting Small

HOLDING YOUR WORK

There are lots of different ways in which the thread and hook can be held for a comfortable crochet experience with even tension. Most of the time it is easier to hold them in the same way as you would when crocheting something bigger, but here are some things that I do that may be useful for crocheting small:

I find the pencil position most comfortable for micro-crochet rather than the knife position (1). This way you can rest your middle finger on top of the loops already on the hook to stop them sliding off or becoming loose, without losing visibility of what you are making.

I wrap the thread around my index finger as shown to give an even tension (2).

I hold a crocheted piece in my non-hook hand with the tip of my thumb and the side of my middle finger for better visibility (3).

I also sometimes use a rubber or plastic thimble for the non-hook hand middle finger. This is particularly good for protecting fingers when using minute hooks and starting a crochet piece that is worked in rows, especially when crocheting onto a foundation row of tiny chain stitches. Alternatively, you can wrap your finger in washi tape, masking tape or a plaster.

STARTING OUT

For those who already love making amigurumi but have never gone small before, I recommend working with a 3mm (D/3) hook and double knitting yarn, and gradually working your way down the hook and thread sizes. If you can't go much smaller than 2mm (B/1), don't worry, your amigurumis will still turn out adorably small.

Experiment with different hook sizes for the thread you are using. Though it is typical to choose a smaller hook for tighter stitches, you may want to try a slightly bigger hook to begin with. There is more information on thread thicknesses in Before You Begin: Tools and Materials.

Choose lighter coloured thread instead of darker ones, as dark threads and stitches can be hard to see.

Remember that the first couple of rounds can be the hardest because that is when your work is at its smallest. Keep going - as your work gets bigger it will be easier to hold and you will conquer those stitches!

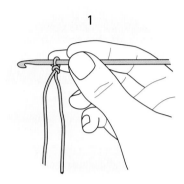

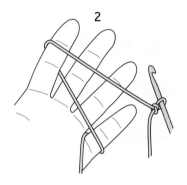

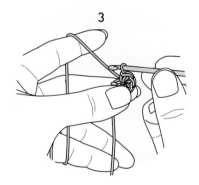

SAVING TIME

Crochet in loose ends when you change colour on an amigurumi project so that there are fewer threads to sew in afterwards. Not only does this save time, but it is often neater and more secure, just pull the excess thread taut before trimming off.

TAKING CARE

A hands-free magnifier would be very useful for beginners, even if you have good eyesight.

Crocheting in a natural light is a given regardless of the size of your crochet projects. I suggest that you work with numerous good lights rather than one intense light source. Not only is it a strain on your eyes, but the smaller hooks are mostly steel and shiny, and the flash of the reflection from an intense light source as the hook moves is distracting and bad for your eyes. In addition to that, a singular directed light can cast shadows from your fingers and thumbs onto your work, which is more pronounced when you are crocheting on such a small scale.

SEWING IN ENDS

John James bead embroidery needles in size 10 are great for sewing in those pesky ends when crocheting with finer threads. They are very strong considering their fineness, and the eye of the needle is slim so the crochet stitches don't stretch as you pass it through.

Crochet Basics

CROCHET STITCH TERMINOLOGY

Each motif in this book has a crochet pattern written in UK crochet terms, sometimes with an accompanying diagram. This table shows what each stitch abbreviation or symbol means alongside the US equivalent where relevant.

Abbreviation	Symbol	UK meaning	US meaning (if different)
ss	●	Slip stitch	same as UK
ch	⬯	Chain stitch	same as UK
dc	✕ ✛	Double crochet	sc Single crochet
dc2tog	 A ⟑	2 double crochet together, used for reducing the amount of stitches on a row or a round	sc2tog 2 single crochet together, used for reducing the amount of stitches on a row or a round
htr	⊤	Half treble crochet	hdc Half double crochet
tr	Ŧ	Treble crochet	dc Double crochet
dtr	Ŧ	Double treble crochet	tr Treble crochet
ttr	Ŧ	Triple treble crochet	dtr Double treble crochet
CL eg. 2trCL, 3trCL	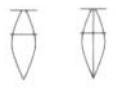 ⬙ ⬙	Cluster stitch	same as UK, but can be added onto US terms eg. 2dcCL, 3dcCL
BO eg. 4trBO, 5trBO, 4dtrBO, 5dtrBO	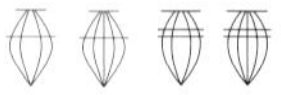 ⬙ ⬙ ⬙ ⬙	Bobble stitch	Same as UK, but can be added onto US terms eg. 4dcBO, 5dcBO, 4trBO, 5trBO
PC	⬙	Popcorn stitch	same as UK
Puff	⬙	Puff stitch	same as UK
BL, BL only eg. 2BLdc	⌒	Crochet into back loop only	same as UK, but can be added onto US terms eg. 2BLsc
FL, FL only eg. 2FLdc	⌣	Crochet into front loop only	same as UK, but can be added onto US terms eg. 2FLsc
Picot eg. 2ch picot	◌◌	Picot stitch	same as UK
Magic ring	◎	Magic ring	same as UK

Here are some additional abbreviations that you will come across in the patterns:

rem: Remaining

sp(s): Space or spaces

st(s): Stitch or stitches

RS: Right side of crochet – this is important if you are turning your crochet and working in rows

WS: Wrong side of crochet

[square brackets]: Crochet a sequence of stitches on repeat or into a specific stitch/space

(brackets): Explains what the crochet should look like at any point in the pattern, or summarises how many stitches you should have at the end of a round

* or **: Repeat a crochet sequence from this marked point (*) in the pattern

READING A CROCHET CHART

Some crocheters like written patterns, some prefer diagrams, and others rely on both. In this book the diagrams are colour coded in black and grey, so it is easier to see and differentiate the rounds. There are also some symbols in red; these are made this colour to set them apart from other rounds in the pattern. This is used to indicate a change in thread colour, an edging, or surface crochet. Look out for the arrows that indicate where a round or row starts.

WORKING IN ROWS

Referring to the pattern to see how many foundation chains are needed (in this pattern it's thirteen) start at (1). Follow the pattern from right to left on the first row (2). Follow the pattern from left to right on the second row (3). Notice the turning chains (4), these could be one to four chain stitches long depending on the height of the crochet stitch that is worked after it. Continue to crochet back and forth to build up the crocheted fabric.

If you are working on a boxy design, such as the popcorn, textbook, or house, you will be adding a chain stitch mid row at some point in the pattern (5). This creates a fold line that defines the edges.

WORKING IN ROUNDS

Crochet diagrams worked in the round start at the centre. You will tend to see this more for patterns that are worked in singular rounds that have a start and a finish with a joining slip stitch, rather than continuous rounds. Look out for the arrows that indicate where a round starts. Notice the spiral in the centre which indicates a magic ring, which is where you start. The example here is the Hull and Base for the Boat in the Travel chapter.

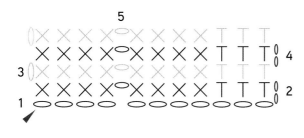

Crochet Techniques

MAGIC CIRCLE OR RING

The magic circle can be tricky but, once mastered, it will be your best friend in micro-crochet. It allows you to quickly start working a shape in the round and you can pull it extra tight so that you don't see an opening. There are lots of different methods to making and holding a magic ring, but I like to crochet my first round with the ring wrapped around my fingers. It really helps with counting stitches, handling, and maintaining tension.

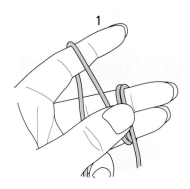
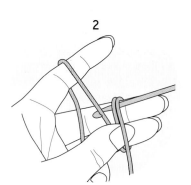

- Wrap the thread round your middle and ring fingers twice (1).

- Place the hook under the 2 threads, yarn-over and pull though (2).

- Crochet the first round of your pattern, keeping your fingers in place for support as long as needed (3).

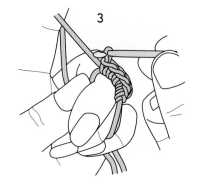
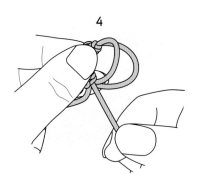

- Remove the hook and your fingers to reveal the the two loops of the magic ring and excess thread. Tug the excess thread (4), one of the loops should begin to shrink. Pick up that loop and pull to draw the other one to a complete close.

- Pull the excess thread again to pull the last loop to a loose close (5). You can then slip stitch into the first stitch or continue to work in continuous rounds.

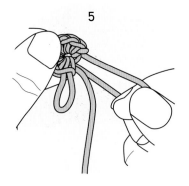

I recommend that you don't pull the magic ring too tight until you start on the next round, otherwise it tightens that first stitch, making it difficult to get your hook through.

For some threads, two loops may not be necessary; I found that 1 loop was more than sufficient for the Scheepjes Sweet Treat cotton thread and the Gütermann top stitching thread. However, anything finer than that would benefit from having 2 loops in your magic ring to make it extra secure.

MAGIC RING ALTERNATIVE

An alternative to the magic ring is crocheting a chain of 6 stitches, slip stitch to join, crochet your first round, then sew around the back of the stitches using the thread end and draw to a close like a drawstring bag.

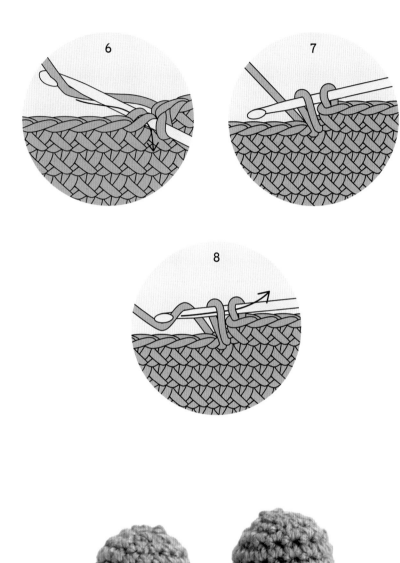

YARNING UNDER VS YARNING OVER

Yarning under refers to a subtle change in making a double crochet (US single crochet) stitch. Crocheters often use this technique because it makes their stitches tighter, so stuffing doesn't show through the stitches. It also requires slightly less yarn per stitch. The photo below demonstrates the differences; traditional yarn-over stitches are 'V' shaped and appear to be stacked in a tilted right position. The yarn-under technique gives an 'X' shape to the stitches, giving them the appearance of being directly stacked on top of each other.

Here is how to work a yarn under:

- Place your hook into your stitch. Hook onto your working yarn. The yarn should be under your hook not wrapped around it (6).

- Pull through for 2 loops on your hook (7).

- Yarn-over (8) and pull through like you would a regular double crochet stitch.

I tend to use both of these techniques in amigurumi, it depends on what I feel like doing on any given day. I tend to yarn-over with super micro-amigurumi and yarn-under with the thicker threads, so please don't think that your work isn't proper amigurumi if you're not adopting this method.

Yarning under   Yarning over

MARKING YOUR STITCHES

Unless you're really good at counting your stitches in your head or out loud when crocheting, I thoroughly recommend marking your stitches. Contrasting scrap thread will be your friend.

- The first thing you need to do is decide whether you want to mark the first or last stitch of the round. It's personal preference, but I like to mark the last stitch of the round.

- Find a contrasting thread and hook it through your last stitch (9). You know you have reached the end of a round in the right place when you crochet into that exact stitch. When you do, hook your thread through the stitch you have just made (10). It looks like a running stitch once you have marked a few rounds using this method.

- If you find this a bit tricky to handle when starting a new project, you can introduce this into the third or fourth round when you have better handling of your work.

- Notice how it twists as you progress through the rounds, this is completely normal. In fact, the fewer stitches you have on a round, the more it will do so (11).

- Once your amigurumi is finished, you can simply trim and pull out your thread (12).

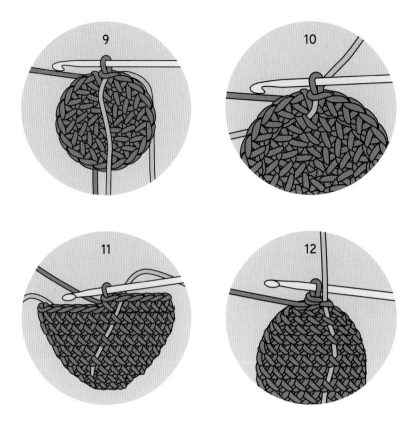

Scrap yarn being used as a stitch marker

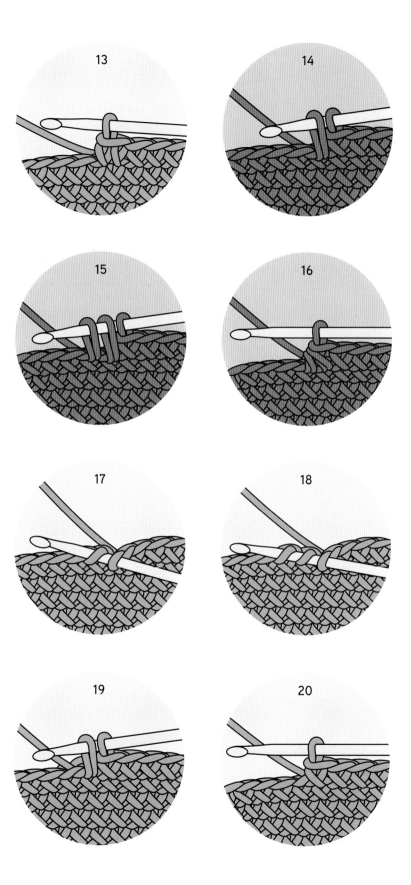

INCREASING & DECREASING STITCHES

To make a simple shape like a ball you need to increase and decrease the number of stitches on any given round. Increasing stitches is straightforward, but you have a couple of options for decreasing stitches, so experiment to see which techniques suit you best:

INCREASING STITCHES

Referred to in a pattern as 'inc' or 2dc in next st.

- Work 2 double crochets into a stitch instead of one, or you may add more than that if the pattern instructs you to do so **(13)**.

DECREASING STITCHES

The option is called dec or dc2tog in patterns. This is a good method for crocheting backwards and forwards in rows. This stitch is a little more noticeable when working in the round, but easier on the hands if you are working super small.

- Place hook into stitch, yarn-over and pull through (2 loops on hook) **(14)**.
- Move onto the next stitch and repeat previous step (3 loops on hook) **(15)**.
- Yarn-over and pull through all loops. You now have one stitch instead of two **(16)**.

INVISIBLE DECREASE

This method is great for amigurumi because you can barely see where a decrease has been worked.

- Place your hook into the FL of next stitch from underneath (2 loops on hook) **(17)**.
- Do the same in the next stitch (3 loops on hook) **(18)**.
- Yarn-over, pull through the 2 FLs (2 loops on hook) **(19)**.
- Yarn-over, pull through rem 2 loops, like a regular double crochet stitch **(20)**.

STARTING & FINISHING ROUNDS FOR STRIPES

The way stripes look on your finished piece can be affected by how you crochet the rounds, either as singular or continuous rounds.

Singular rounds create concentric circles. They are less popular than continuous rounds as you can easily see the joins of each round. To join a round, you need to slip stitch into the first stitch then make a chain to begin the next round, the extra slip stitch and chain stitch are what makes it visible. However, this is a good method when making coloured stripes because the ends meet.

The other method is working in **continuous rounds**. The rounds created by this method look like a spiral. It is popular because there are no visible joins and the overall look is neater. However, when adding stripes to your work it gives a staggered effect which is not always desirable.

Here are a few tips on starting and finishing a round when making stripes in singular rounds:

STARTING

- Make a slip stitch and place the loop onto your hook as if you are starting a chain stitch (**21**).
- Place your hook into the first stitch of the previous round (**22**).
- Yarn-over and pull through the stitch (**23**).
- Yarn-over and pull through the remaining loops on the hook (**24**).

FINISHING

- Place the hook into the last stitch, yarn-over and pull through like you would a regular stitch (2 loops on hook) (**25**).
- Place the hook into the first stitch of the round (**26**).
- Yarn-over and pull through all stitches and loops. Make a chain to begin the next round (**27**).
- If you need to change colour, yarn-over and pull the new colour through all the new stitches and loops (**28**).

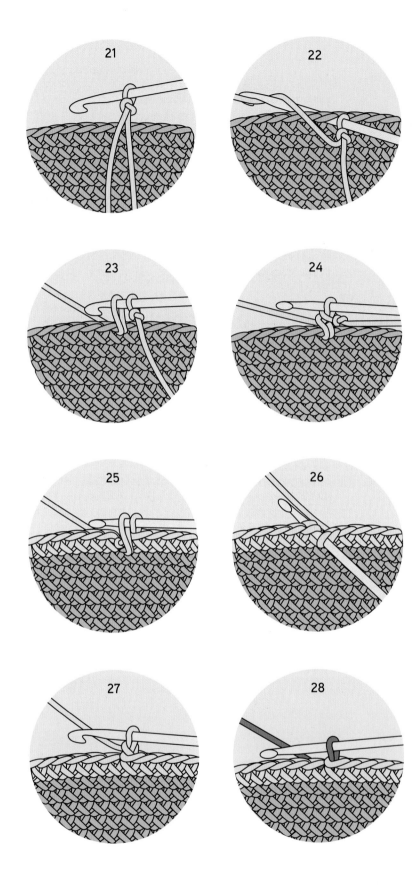

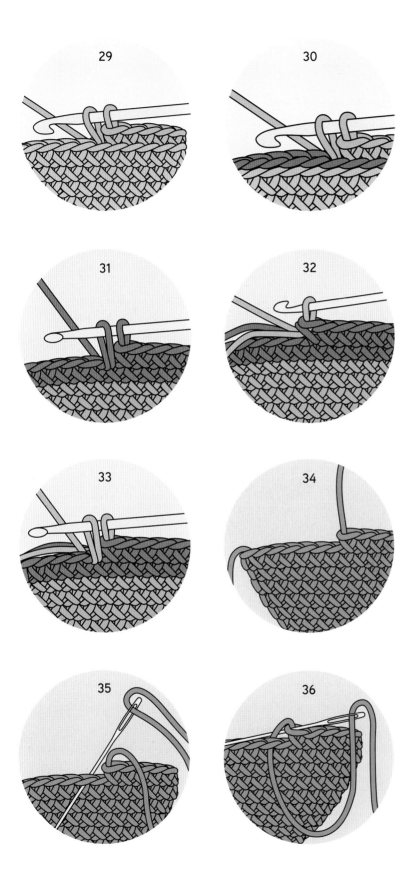

ADDING STRIPES USING THE BACK LOOPS

Here are some different effects in stripes that can be achieved depending on the placement of the double crochet stitches:

- Have a go at crocheting into the BLs only for a crisp edge **(29)**.

- Alternatively, you can do loose slip stitches into the back loops of the round, then crochet into the back loops of the slip stitches and the round together. Work the row of slip stitches in a different colour for a cheeky added stripe **(30)**!

CHANGING COLOUR HALFWAY THROUGH A ROW OR ROUND

The principle of changing colour halfway through a row is the same as in standard-sized crochet. It begins in the stitch before the colour change.

Make a stitch as you usually would, stopping before the last yarn-over, and pull through **(31)**. Swap colours on the last yarn-over-pull-through to complete the colour change, then use that colour for the next stitch or stitches **(32 & 33)**.

THE INVISIBLE SLIP STITCH

Finishing on an edge or a last round, this works well on singular and continuous rounds.

- Complete last stitch as usual.

- Trim yarn and pull the thread all the way through the top of the stitch **(34)**.

- Thread the yarn through the second stitch of the round (skip the first stitch) **(35)**.

- Thread yarn through, back into the centre of the last stitch, imitating the tops of stitches **(36)**.

CROCHETING ARMS & FEET/LEGS USING BOBBLE STITCHES

Adding bobble stitches to a round is a good way to add arms and legs without having to crochet extra components and sew them onto the body. It is made by crocheting 4-5 near-complete treble crochet stitches into one stitch, and drawing them all together, which makes a squishy ball shape. The stitch is very similar in construction to a cluster stitch (CL), which is made by crocheting fewer treble crochet stitches together in the same fashion.

In the patterns of this book, it is written as 4trBO, 5trBO, 4dtrBO or 5dtrBO. The '4tr'/'4dtr' part refers to how many part-finished treble/double treble crochet stitches are required. The more there are in your bobble stitch, the puffier the overall look will be. This is how to crochet a 4trBO:

- Make a regular treble crochet (US double crochet) stitch, but stop at the very last yarn-over, pull through. You should have 2 loops on your hook (37).

- Do not complete this stitch, instead repeat the process three more times into the same stitch (38). Repeat once more for a 5trBO.

- It should look like this, five loops on the hook (39).

- Yarn-over and pull through all loops (40).

- Make a chain stitch to secure, then continue the round using regular double crochet stitches (41).

- When crocheting above the bobble stitch in the next round, 1dc in the bobble stitch just before the chain stitch, skip the chain within the bobble stitch, then dc in the next dc of previous rounds as normal. This squashes the bobble stitch and makes it look more pronounced (42 & 43).

OTHER BOBBLE STITCH METHODS

You can also make separate bobble stitches for cute limbs, stubby ears or tails, which can be sewn onto a finished body that has already been stuffed. If you prefer this method to crocheting bobbles into the amigurumi body, swap a bobble stitch for a standard double crochet stitch in any of the patterns in this book.

You can start a separate a bobble stitch in three different ways: by making a magic ring, by making a chain stitch, or by crocheting into the front loop (FL) of a double crochet stitch on the main body.

Here's the pattern:

Make a magic ring or 1ch, 3ch, 4trBO in magic ring, fasten off (44).

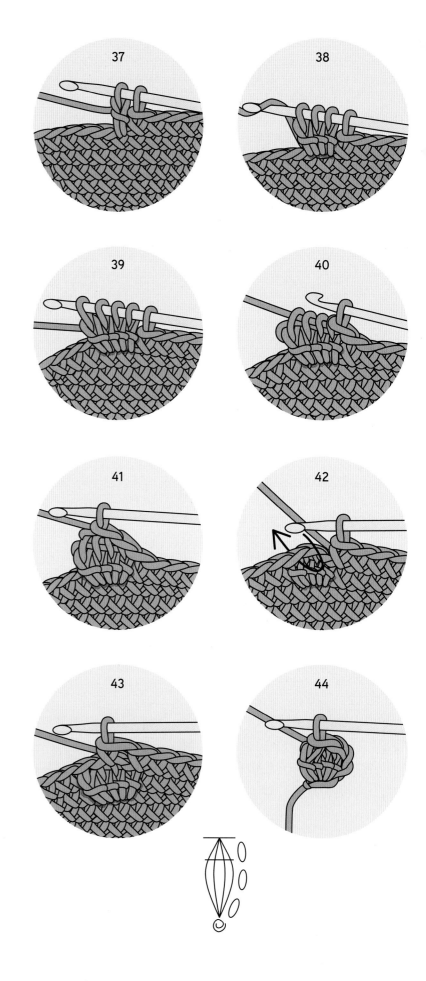

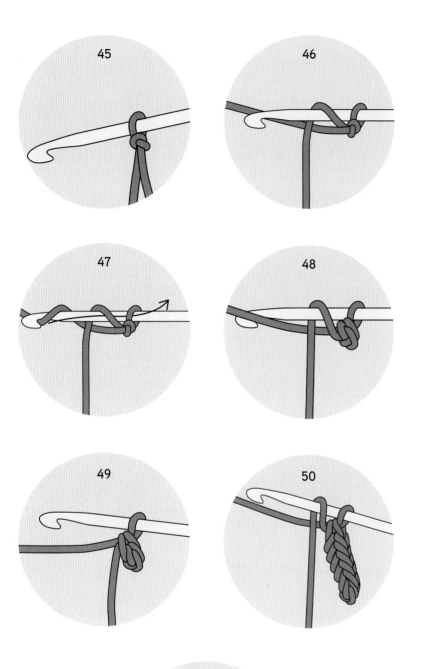

PERFECT CROCHET I-CORD (PCIC)

Sometimes you need to be able to crochet something long and thin, like an arm, a leg or a tail, which would be too fiddly to crochet in continuous rounds of double crochet stitches. This is where the Crochet Long Tail Foundation Base Chain or Perfect Crochet I-Cord can be very useful. In this book it is referred to as PCIC and it was first invented by Melissa of Mellow Me Creations. It is a method for creating long thin elements with more structural integrity than a row of chain then double crochet stitches. Though it is being used for amigurumi in this book, it can also be used like a row of foundation double crochet stitches, so has other applications such as on clothing, blankets, and accessories like handbag straps. Sometimes when you create a row of chain stitches to start a row or round, it can appear gappy depending on your tension – this stitch is a good replacement to resolve that issue.

This is how it's done:

- Reserve a long length of thread for the tail. Make a slip knot on your hook like any other regular crochet stitch (45).

- Wrap the tail end over your hook, from the front, upwards then away from you (46).

- Yarn-over with your working yarn and pull through (47).

- Wrap the tail over your hook again (48).

- Yarn-over, pull through (49).

- Repeat the process as per the pattern or until you reach desired length (50).

ALTERNATIVE

One alternative to the PCIC is working a row of chain stitches, then crocheting a row of double crochet stitches into the back loop of the chain stitches. This gives an identical and consistent appearance to both sides of the strip just made (51).

FORWARD KNOT

Think back to friendship bracelets when you were at school, the forward knot wraps around other threads to create thin lengths that have a bit of rigidity, much like the PCIC. This is used in the birthday cake pattern, and you can use it to make lengths that are also stripey as in the milkshake pattern.

Start with 2 lengths of thread in alternating colours if you want to add a stripe, make an overhand knot in the middle of one length, thread the other thread through the knot before tightening, trapping it in the knot.

Pin the lengths by the knot onto something stable. I like to do this on my knee with the thread pinned to my jeans.

Wrap one thread over the top of the other threads then round behind, making a loop. Thread the end through the loop and tighten, trapping the other threads **(52)**. Repeating this process will make a length of knots that has a ridge that spirals around it. Swap over the threads to change the colour.

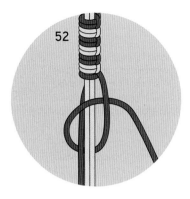

WHIPPED RUNNING STITCH

This is a good way of making sewing outlines that are without gaps on a crocheted surface, such as waistbands, as on the gnome in the Myth & Legend chapter.

Make a length of running stitches, then feed the needle back through the stitches from the same direction, filling in the gaps as you go along **(53)**.

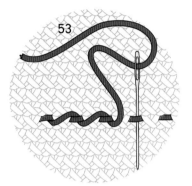

BOBBLE STITCH

See Crocheting Arms & Feet/Legs Using Bobble Stitches.

CLUSTER STITCH

The cluster stitch is very similar in construction to a bobble stitch. It is made by crocheting 2-3 near-complete treble crochet stitches into one stitch and drawing them all together with a yarn over and pull through. It is used in the hair for the Fairy and Merman in the Myth & Legend chapter along with puff stitches to give a wavy texture to the crochet. In a crochet pattern it is abbreviated to CL and can be written as 2trCL or 3trCL, depending on how many treble crochet stitches are needed. This is how to crochet a 3trCL:

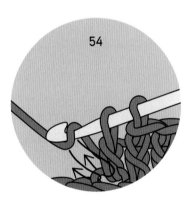

- Make a regular treble crochet stitch, but stop at the very last yarn over, pull through. You should have 2 loops on your hook. Do not complete this stitch, instead repeat the process two more times into the same stitch **(54)**. Only repeat once for a 2trCL.

- Yarn-over and pull through all loops **(55)**.

PUFF STITCH

Crochet puff stitches are also similar to bobble stitches. They are a little trickier to make at first because you have to keep a lot of loops on your hook, but they create a lovely smooth finish that is really cute for little arms and feet. Like the bobble stitch you can incorporate them into the body of your amigurumi or make them separately and sew them after stuffing.

- Yarn over, insert hook in stitch, yarn over, pull through a long loop (56).
- Repeat this process 4 more times. If you can only do 3 in micro crochet that's fine, you'll still get a nice puff shape (57).
- Yarn over, pull through all loops (1 loop left on hook). Make a chain stitch to secure the loops (58).

PICOT STITCH

A picot stitch is a simple way of adding a point to a flat crocheted shape, such as a leaf or a wing. It involves making 2 or 3 chain stitches, depending on what the pattern requires, then making a slip stitch into a previous stitch. The slip stitch placement is important; insert the hook into the middle of the stitch from above, in between the front and back loop (59).

SS, 1CH EDGING

A simple [ss, 1ch] in each stitch is an edging that gives a beautiful plaited effect and can also be used to join components of an amigurumi together. This technique is used for the ice cream cone and milkshake in the Food chapter.

SURFACE CROCHET

This can be worked on flat work and 3D pieces and makes a nice alternative to embroidery or crocheting stripes into a shape. It is a slip stitch across a surface rather than an edge. You can 'hook' the yarn from either below the crochet piece or above, which is easier when working on amigurumi that have already been stuffed. This technique is used for the satchel fastenings in the Back to School chapter.

Finishing Techniques

EMBROIDERING FACES

Adding eyes and a tiny mouth can transform a formless blob of crochet into the cutest thing you've ever made. Here are a few things to consider when adding faces.

PROPORTION MATTERS

Ever wondered what makes a face cute? Broadly speaking, it's the size and spacing of the eyes and the forehead. The bigger the forehead, the younger and 'cuter' your amigurumi will look.

EXPRESSION

You don't have to stick to round eyes in amigurumi, so consider different shapes for different expressions, such as little 'V' and 'U' shapes which can be used for both eyes and mouths. Consider adding cheeks, lashes, freckles or even eyebrows.

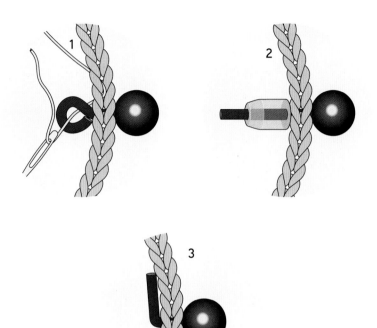

USING PIN EYES

There are several ways that you can attach pin eyes to your amigurumi. These are great for tiny crochet using lace weight threads such as the Scheepjes Sweet Treat yarn used in this book. I recommend using pliers and trying out these methods on a scrap piece of crochet to work out which one is best for you.

METHOD 1

Before stuffing your amigurumi, thread the eye through your crochet, bend the wire into a loop with pliers, then sew to the inside of your amigurumi with a matching cotton thread (1).

METHOD 2

Use a rubber earring back, bend the wire then cut the excess off with pliers. This method is a bit bulkier and will take up more space on the inside of your crocheted head or body. However, it is quicker and less fiddly than the other methods. You can further reinforce the eyes by carefully adding a dot of superglue to the earring back once finished (2).

METHOD 3

After stuffing your amigurumi, make an 'L' shape with pliers then wiggle it through your crochet. Feel for the wire underneath the surface of the fabric and secure from the outside with matching cotton thread. This is a good method if, like me, you prefer to add your eyes at the end of a finished amigurumi rather than halfway through making it before stuffing. Do keep in mind that this can be a tricky process if you have stuffed your crochet with dense yarn scraps, as it is harder to wiggle the pin eye through the fabric (3).

EMBROIDERING EYES

My favourite technique is the French knot, as it's quick and gives a round shape. You can embroider before or after stuffing, but I prefer embroidering afterwards. I recommend you practise it before you commit it to your amigurumi, as mistakes are not easily undone – you would have to snip them off.

Whether I am embroidering eyes or beading them, this is how I like to start:

· Thread the needle into the head where you want one eye to be and back out where the other eye needs to be, leaving lengths for embroidery on both ends (**4 & 5**).

· Though you will be embroidering with this thread, this method acts as a place marker and you can check positioning of the eyes before doing any extra sewing.

HOW TO MAKE A FRENCH KNOT

· Thread the cotton through your amigurumi where you want to eye to be (**6**).

· Wrap thread around the needle, twice for small knot, three times for a large knot (**7**).

· Keeping the working thread taut so that the knot does not loosen, push the needle through the knots and your amigurumi (**8**).

The knot should be tight and round (**9**).

ALTERNATIVE - TINY SATIN STITCH

This is essentially making a small stitch that is repeatedly done in the same place to build up shape. This is good if you want oval eyes or eyes of a different shape to circles. You need to make the same number of stitches to each eye to maintain evenness and symmetry. Make sure that the stitches sit in the same direction for an even satin-like surface (**10**).

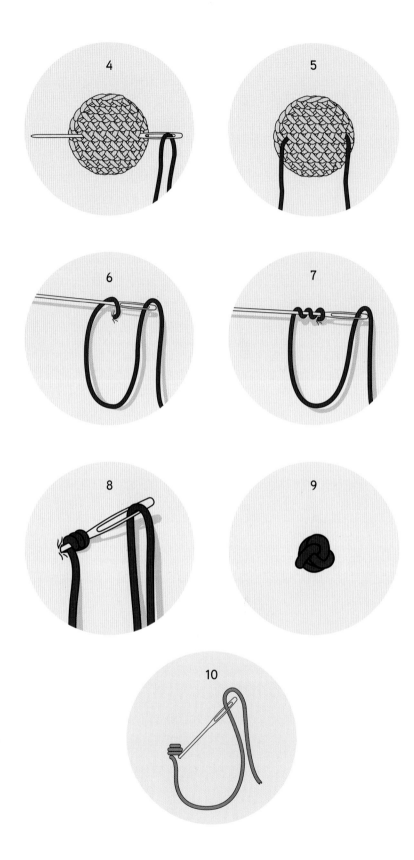

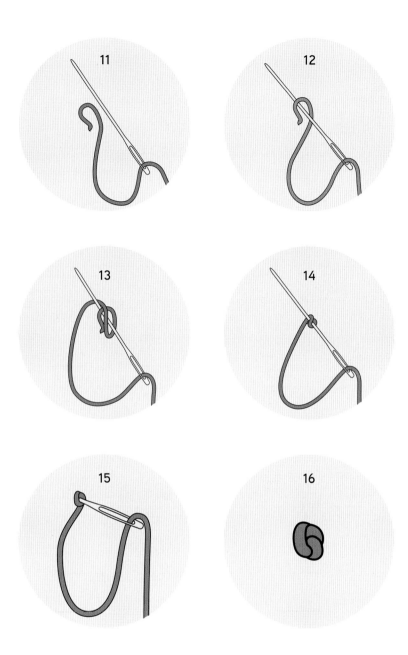

HOW TO MAKE A COLONIAL KNOT

The Colonial knot is like the bigger sibling to the French knot. There are more steps, but once perfected you can achieve nice round eyes for your amigurumi. Here is how to do it:

- Like the French knot, thread the cotton out of your amigurumi where you want your eye to be (**11**).

- Make a little 'hill' with the working thread, place the needle through the 'hill', taking the working yarn underneath the needle (**12**).

- Bring the working thread up, and wrap around the needle as shown (**13**).

- Tighten the working thread so the loops are snug around the needle (**14**).

- Keeping the thread tight, thread the needle back through your amigurumi at the eye position (**15 & 16**).

HAIR

Personally, I prefer making hair with rounds of crochet, before sewing it on, as you can see on the merman and fairy in the Myth & Legend chapter. However, there is a way you can add hair to tiny heads when it simply must be long and flowing, such as on a mermaid or a wizard.

- Starting at the front hairline, make a running stitch along the crown of the head, or further if you're making pigtails (17).

- Take the thread end from the front of the crown and repeat this method, weaving through the head in opposite directions to make continuous figures of 8. This makes the parting and foundation to attach the hair (18).

- Using a needle and long lengths of yarn, thread through the figure of 8 in big loops. Wrap round a piece of card to prevent tangling and to maintain consistent lengths. Repeat on the other side of the parting (19).

- Remove the card and trim the loops at the bottom to make the lengths. The threads still aren't secure, so be careful not to pull on the strands (20).

- Arrange the hair how you prefer; as a braid, a bun or simply tied at the back. Make sure that the hair is up in some sort of style, otherwise the hair strands can be easily pulled out (21).

- Alternatively, you can work this process on the front of the hair, then make repeated long stitches on the rest of the head to give a similar effect. This was used for the mermaid in the Myth & Legend chapter.

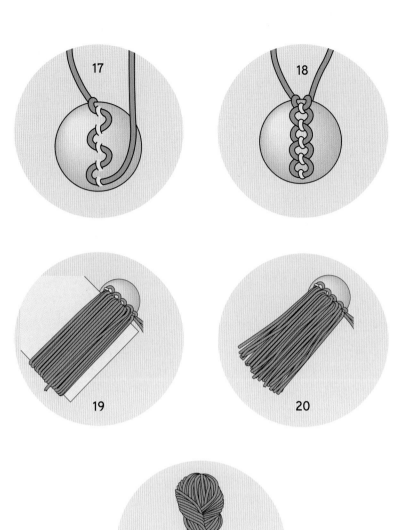

STUFFING

When working small, you have a few more options with regards to stuffing your crochet pieces, mainly because you haven't got much to stuff! Here are a few options that you can try out to see what suits you best.

TOY STUFFING/POLYESTER FILLER

Though great for squishiness, especially for large amigurumi pieces, it's not my first recommendation. I have found that it can catch and wrap around the hook in an irritating way, especially on the last 1 or 2 rounds when you are reducing your stitches. There's nothing worse than finishing a piece only to find those tiny yet indestructible fibres sticking out of a sewn-up hole or intertwined with a stitch.

SCRAP YARN

This is my favourite type of stuffing and is what I used for all the pieces in this book. You can use acrylic yarn for squishiness, but I lean more towards cotton. With cotton, the more you stuff, the more dense and solid your amigurumi will feel. You can even use cotton that matches the colour of your amigurumi if you're worried about visible gaps in your work.

When it comes to especially small pieces, I find that thread ends that come from the magic ring of round 1 is enough stuffing, especially when it comes to narrow pieces such as legs on an amigurumi doll.

When stuffing with yarn, I recommend inserting the ends with tweezers first, then the rest of the thread. That way, you can avoid the annoying frayed fibres that can get tangled up in your last rounds, much like the toy stuffing does.

SOLID REINFORCEMENTS

Card or thin plastic are fantastic for maintaining the shape of more geometrically shaped amigurumis, as they keep surfaces flat and edges crisp. You can cut them to size and tack to the inside of a crochet piece before stuffing and sewing up. Reinforcements can be made from card, foldable plastic that is used in stationery (think plastic binder or notepad covers), or clean food packaging. A good example of this in use are the blocky cuboid buildings in the About Town chapter. I used cardboard from a chocolates gift box, simply trimmed down to size with scissors, with no fancy measuring or equipment, then used the thread ends from the embroidery to sew them in place from the inside. Make the pieces slightly smaller than your crocheted panels so that they don't interfere with sewing around the edges.

You can use other objects within your stuffing to add stability and weight where standard stuffing cannot, such as buttons or beads. I found that a small shirt button was perfect for the tree in the About Town chapter. The design is very top-heavy, so inserting a button into the base of the trunk kept it flat and prevented it from toppling over.

WIRE AND PIPE CLEANERS

Wire is commonly used in dollmaking and amigurumi, and you can use it for micro-crochet too. I like to use pipe cleaners because they're readily available from most craft stores and the fuzzy fibres act as stuffing at the same time. You can twist two together and roll them up to fill bulkier parts of an amigurumi. I used pipe cleaners in the dragon, dolphin and the sea serpent, so that the necks and the tails can be posable.

I recommend folding in the ends when inserting them into your amigurumi so that they can't poke through any stitches.

Project Ideas

The nice thing about micro-amigurumi is there are many sneaky ways you can incorporate them into your everyday life. Here are some quick ways that you can adapt your amigurumis for different uses:

SNEAKY MESSENGERS

This is great for slightly bigger amigurumi – crochet a little patch and sew it onto your chosen amigurumi, leaving an opening so that you can sneak hidden messages and hide them around the house. I thoroughly recommend the owl design for this as it already has a belly just waiting for a pocket!

DECORATIONS

Add loops to the top of your work to make decorations, whether it be for a children's room, a birthday or another festive occasion. You can even thread string through a chapter's worth of amigurumi to make bunting.

BOOKMARKS

Add ribbon or a chain of crochet to make a bookmark.

Don't forget that you can scale up these patterns with any yarn, have a go at crocheting your crochet pieces using DK or fluffy velvet yarn!

JEWELLERY AND KEYRINGS

Of course, there is always jewellery! Sew jump rings to the top of your amis to attach findings such as ear wires or bails for pendants. Turn your amigurumis into charms by adding bracelet clasps, so that they can be hooked onto anything from zip-up jackets to pencil cases.

MAGNETS

You can buy super small magnets online and stitch them inside your amigurumi before you stuff them. Stick them on your fridge or decorate your message boards!

About the Author

Steffi is a jewellery maker and crochet pattern designer in North Yorkshire, England. She specialises in micro-crochet and draws inspiration from the natural world, vintage textile pieces and nostalgic crochet heirlooms such as granny square blankets. She has a multidisciplinary background in metalwork, textiles, ceramics and laser cutting, having graduated in 2013 with a degree in Design Crafts from De Montfort University.

Suppliers

Duttons for Buttons for Gütermann threads, bookmark ribbons, John James needles, jewellery findings and toy stuffing.
duttonsforbuttons.co.uk, 01904 632042

Gillies Fabrics for Gütermann threads.
gilliesfabrics.co.uk, 01904 626244

Wool Warehouse for Gütermann threads, DMC threads and crochet cotton, Scheepjes Sweet Treat cotton threads, Anchor threads, and Clover and Tulip crochet hooks.
woolwarehouse.co.uk

DMC for crochet cotton, embroidery threads and crochet threads. Based in France.
DMC.co.uk

Amazon shops for 2mm agate beads, pin eyes, jewellery pliers and stuffing.
amazon.co.uk

Thanks

To my family, Mum and Dennis, Kate, Kirsty, Matthew, Jon and Sarah, Joanne, Cag and Mick, John and Irene.

To the Lumley's Legends, Kathryn, Martin, Izzy, Kerry, Kim, Charlotte, Bev and Carolyn. Thank you for keeping my spirits high as I worked my way through teaching and writing this book.

To Tanya, John, and the ladies at Duttons for Buttons, thank you for the lunchbreak chats, help with threads, and your overall warmth and kindness. To Katy, Amy and Megan, thank you for your encouragement!

To everyone at David and Charles, thank you so much for helping me write a second book! It's been a new adventure and I have loved every second of it.

Index

This book has been printed on paper from approved
suppliers and made from pulp from sustainable sources.

Printed in China through Asia Pacific Offset for:
David and Charles, Ltd
Suite A, Tourism House, Pynes Hill, Exeter, EX2 5WS

10 9 8 7 6 5 4 3 2

Publishing Director: Ame Verso
Senior Commissioning Editor: Sarah Callard
Managing Editor: Jeni Chown
Editor: Jessica Cropper
Project Editor: Carol Ibbetson
Head of Design: Anna Wade
Designer: Lucy Ridley
Pre-press Designer: Ali Stark
Illustrations: Kuo Kang Chen
Art Direction: Prudence Rogers
Photography: Jason Jenkins
Production Manager: Beverley Richardson

David and Charles publishes high-quality books on
a wide range of subjects. For more information visit
www.davidandcharles.com.

Share your makes with us on social media using
#dandcbooks and follow us on Facebook and Instagram
by searching for @dandcbooks.

Layout of the digital edition of this book may vary
depending on reader hardware and display settings.